BISHOPSTONE WITH LITTLE HINTON PARISH

ITS ARCHAEOLOGY AND HISTORY

DEDICATION

This book is dedicated to the all the inhabitants of Bishopstone and Little Hinton who are keeping the peacefulness and communal spirit alive within the Parish and those who strive to protect its glorious countryside and wildlife.

ACKNOWLEDGEMENTS

The authors would like to thank Nick Boon for his superb cartoons and the various landowners and tenants who freely allowed us to wander the land and dig holes in search of the Parish's ancient past.

Bishopstone with Little Hinton Parish

its Archaeology and History

MOGS BOON
and
BERNARD PHILLIPS

THE HOBNOB PRESS

First published in the United Kingdom in 2021

by The Hobnob Press,
8 Lock Warehouse,
Severn Road, Gloucester GL1 2GA
www.hobnobpress.co.uk

© Moggs Boon and Bernard Phillips, 2021

All rights reserved. No part of this book may be reprinted or reproduced or utilised in any form or by any electronic, mechanical or other means, now known or hereafter invented, including photocopying, or in any information storage or retrieval system, without the permission in writing from the copyright holders or their heirs.

British Library Cataloguing in Publication Data
A catalogue record for this book is available from the British Library

ISBN 978-1-914407-20-8

Typeset in Scala 11/14 pt.
Typesetting and origination by John Chandler

Front cover: Excavating a medieval building, north of Bishopstone Church

Back cover (main image): Bronze Age round barrow on Hinton Down: and a sixth-century Saxon saucer brooch from Bone Hill.

Contents

Dedication ii
Acknowledgements ii
The Authors vi
Illustrations ix
Maps xi

1. Introduction — 1
2. Topography and Geology — 5
3. British Palaeolithic — 6
4. Mesolithic — 10
5. Neolithic — 14
6. Bronze Age — 19
7. Iron Age — 25
8. Romano-British — 30
9. Late Roman /Anglo Saxon — 39
10. Early Medieval — 47
11. Medieval — 51
12. Post-Medieval — 68
13. Undated Earthworks and Cropmarks — 85
14. The End, or is it? — 87

Further Reading 88
Glossary of Terms 88
Bibliography 90
Notes 93
People and Places Index 95

The Authors

How it all began

Many years ago, having nothing better to do on the bleak Monday evenings of winter, I was persuaded to take a course in A level archaeology. One of our first tasks was to choose a topic on which to base our dissertation. Such was our ignorance that most of the class plumped for studying something exotic, such as Stonehenge, because everything has been discovered, hasn't it? Purely because I could not afford the petrol for a long trip, I cast around for something within walking distance. During a chance conversation with an old farmer, I learned that there were a few remains of an old water mill less than a mile to the north of my cottage, not exactly glamorous but it would do. Oh yes, and he had an old map. Great, I adore maps and spent happy hours poring over it (OK I am an anorak). The project was fascinating, I learned a bit about water mills and found there was plenty of material for my exam topic. But back to the map, it showed all the fields in Hinton Parish and their names. I was interested to see a strip of land called Millbank on the stream below the Manor. The farmer assured me that there had never been a mill, but I had to go and see for myself. Not immediately, there was a bull in the field. I was told that it was friendly, it will chase you, but it only wants to play. A theory I was not about to test. I waited until it had moved on to pastures new. Another thing for which I waited was to be accompanied by a real archaeologist, who knew what he was doing. As it happened, I knew one, Bernard Phillips. And that was the beginning of our joint exploration of the parish. Yes, indeed there had been a mill, the huge stones that had been a dam were still visible in the bank and there were records of at least two different mills in the parish. One Saturday night, I lay by the fire reading Mick Aston's *Interpreting the Landscape* (I told you I am an anorak). When I had the revelation, describing Saxon parish boundaries Mick (yes, the lovely guy from Time Team who wore stripy sweaters) tells us that they tended to follow features, like water ways and if they deviated oddly, it could be to include something important like a mill. I rushed to my office to check on the map. The old Hinton parish boundary ran northwest to southeast following the stream and then did a sudden dog leg to include the strip called, Mill Fields. The Saxon boundary (about which more later) deviated to respect the mill. Oh wow! Within a few months of studying archaeology, I had rediscovered a forgotten site. Much to my surprise I achieved my A level and now I wanted to do some real archaeology. My tutor introduced me to Gary Lock who was directing the Oxford University Archaeological Society dig at Alfred's Castle, Ashbury, which proved to be an extremely exciting site that produced evidence of occupation from the late Bronze Age to Romano British. I also spent several summers excavating a Roman fort at Alchester, near Bicester.

Mogs Boon

Mogs and I met whilst I and a colleague were cataloguing archaeological finds in a temporary storage unit in Swindon. From then on, we became firm friends and colleagues, with her ably helping me on various archaeological contracts in the County, as well as conducting fieldwork in and around Bishopstone and Little Hinton. I have been involved with archaeology in the area since the mid-1960s. Having joined the newly formed Swindon Archaeological Society I eventually became its Field Director. As such I directed and recorded excavations on Roman villas at Stanton Fitzwarren and Starveall Farm in Bishopstone Parish, other minor research excavations, conducted field walking and rescue excavations, notably for the latter during construction of the M4 motorway, Stratton bypass and Lyncroft estate. In 1976 I joined an archaeological team who were excavating in Old Town, Swindon led by the then County Archaeologist Roy Canham. This excavation on the site of Swindon House revealed much about Old Swindon's origins that evidently spanned a period of over ten thousand years. Most important was the discovery of Roman and Saxon buildings. During the summer of 1976 I acted as a supervisor for an archaeological excavation on a Roman town at Lower Wanborough. Returning to the Swindon House excavation I directed its final stages. Two further excavations followed in Old Town with me acting as director and recorder – Lloyds Bank in 1977 and Britannia Place in 1978. The former uncovered the remains of a Saxon hut and Roman building traces, the latter a row of early nineteenth century cottages. These excavations were carried out under the auspices of the County Archaeologist and Wiltshire Archaeological Society. Commencement of an archaeological excavation at Littlecote Park near Hungerford, with me acting as Excavation Director, began in 1978. Open to public viewing this long-term excavation (1978-1993) was paid for initially through the estate owner and subsequently became self-financing, having a museum, tearoom, educational facilities, and a gift shop. The excavation, initially aimed at a Roman villa discovered in the eighteenth century, revealed the site to be multi-period and resulted in the uncovering and recording of a Roman military invasion road, an early Roman settlement of circular huts, an almost entire Roman villa complex, a third of a medieval deserted village (tenth to fifteenth century) and a mid-seventeenth to late-eighteenth-century hunting lodge along with its gardens and river frontage. Following the termination of the Littlecote excavation I undertook freelance archaeological work throughout much of Wiltshire but chiefly in the Swindon area. This has involved work for various companies and individuals as well as Wiltshire County Council Heritage and Libraries, and Swindon Borough Council. Amongst these has been work on the Roman villa/temple site at Abbey Meads in North Swindon, the Saxon/medieval town of Cricklade, an Iron Age and Roman settlement at Calstone near Calne, a Mesolithic to Bronze Age occupation site at Kingsdown Crematorium, Neolithic pits at Whittonditch and a walled eighteenth-century garden at Lydiard Park, Swindon.

Bernard Phillips

Illustrations

Fig. 1. The authors pondering on their next move (Nick Boon)
Fig. 2. Saxon sarsen stone boundary marker on Hinton Downs
Fig. 3. Monks walking the boundary of the spurious charter (Nick Boon)
Fig. 4. Fossil of a clam, from north of Bishopstone Church, of the mid-Cretaceous period
Fig. 5. Late Palaeolithic flint scraper/piercer found north of Little Hinton
Fig. 6. Mesolithic flints from Russley
Fig. 7. An earthen long barrow on the Wanborough/Liddington parish boundary
Fig. 8. Prehistoric Struck Flint Tools from Hinton Manor
Fig. 9. Neolithic polished flint axe head from near Charlbury Hill
Fig. 10. Bronze Age bowl barrow on Hinton Downs
Fig. 11. Bronze dagger from Old town, Swindon (length 11.5cms)
Fig. 12. City Corner, Little Hinton ring ditch excavation
Fig. 13. Late Neolithic/Early Bronze Age flint tools from North of Bishopstone Church
Fig. 14. Liddington Castle, Iron Age hill fort
Fig. 15. Model of an Iron Age hut (Swindon Museum)
Fig. 16. Gold Stater of the East Wiltshire Tribe
Fig. 17. Fragment of decorated bone weaving comb from Russley Downs
Fig. 18. Starveall Farm Roman Villa House Excavation 1972
Fig. 19. Surviving mosaic flooring at Starveal Farm Villa
Fig. 20. Mosaic fragment, from Starveal Farm Villa, depicting a hound.
Fig. 21. Painted wall plaster from Starveall Farm Villa
Fig. 22. Holywell, Little Hinton, location of an ancient medicinal spring
Fig. 23. Drawing of Roman pottery from Holy Well, Little Hinton; rims from a jar, beaker, and lid
Fig. 24. Excavating a Roman pottery kiln at Whitehill Farm, West Swindon
Fig. 25. Liddington Castle Iron Age hillfort was refortified in the fifth century AD
Fig. 26. Anglo-Saxon grass tempered pottery
Fig. 27. Excavation of a Saxon sunken hut in Old Town, Swindon
Fig. 28. Anglo-Saxon saucer brooch from Bone Hill field
Fig. 29. King Alfred the Great
Fig. 30. Sarsen boundary marker, the Har Stan, on Hinton Downs
Fig. 31. St. Mary's Church, Bishopstone
Fig. 32. Twelfth century carved stone corbel on the church's south interior wall
Fig. 33. Sundial on the south exterior wall of Bishopstone Church
Fig. 34. St. Swithun's Church, Hinton

Fig. 35. Drawings of/and actual Medieval tiles in St. Swithun's Church, apart from the 19th century tile (bottom right) from St. Mary's *Bishopstone*

Fig. 36. Details from the font showing a bird and a wolf with a vine issuing from its mouth and an entwined serpent, fish and birds

Fig. 37. Test pit revealing the foundations of St Swithun's Church

Fig. 38. Medieval overshot mill depicted in the fourteenth century Luttrell Psalter

Fig. 39. Thirteenth century manuscript depicting a rat and a cat

Fig. 40. Late 13th to late 14th Century building at Bishopstone with an Infant burial in the corner

Fig. 41. Medieval manuscript depicting a blacksmith's smithy

Fig. 42. 'Ridge and Furrow' strip fields in pasture in nearby Liddington Parish

Fig. 43. Medieval silver coins from Bishopstone

Fig. 44. Rim profiles of Medieval pottery from north of Bishopstone Church

Fig. 45. Fragments of medieval pottery from a kiln site at Minety in North Wiltshire

Fig. 46. Andrews and Dury's map of 1773

Fig. 47. Little Hinton c.1890 showing the five farms that constituted the village

Fig. 48. Boundary stone marked with the letter S near Little Hinton

Fig. 49. Bishopstone Mill building, dated 1818

Fig. 50. Remains of Bishopstone's Mill iron mill wheel and drive shaft

Fig. 51. Remains of the stone dam across the Smal Broc at Mill Bank, Hinton

Fig. 52. Earthworks at Mill Bank, Hinton, and location of the excavation trenches

Fig. 53. Records of Mills in Little Hinton Parish (various sources)

Fig. 54. Overgrown brick channelling of the leat bringing water to Berry Mill, Hinton

Fig, 55. The Tudor Muster of Arms at Bishopstone (Nick Boon)

Fig. 56. The gravestone of Thomas Wallrond 1653

Fig. 57. Seventeenth/Eighteenth century pottery sherds, with wasters, from the Ashton Keynes kiln site

Fig. 58. Mid-Seventeenth to early Eighteenth-Century clay pipe bowls

Maps

1. Topography and Paleontology
2. British Palaeolithic (800,000+ to 10,000 years before present)
3. Mesolithic (8,000 BC – 4,000 BC)
4. Neolithic (4,000 BC – 2,600 BC)
5. Bronze Age (2,600-700 BC)
6. Iron Age (700BC to AD43)
7. Romano-British (AD 43-450)
8. Late Roman/Anglo Saxon (AD 420-850)
9. Early Medieval/Medieval (AD 850-1485)
10. Post-Medieval (1485 – 1900)

Fig. 1. *The authors pondering on their next move (Nick Boon)*

I
Introduction

Over the past twenty years the authors have been involved with archaeological fieldwork and excavation within Bishopstone with Hinton Parish. This parish, until 1934 comprised two parishes – Hinton and Bishopstone. They have an exceptionally long recorded history, to which archaeological discoveries add to and extend the story back many thousands of years.

Little Hinton

The creation of Hinton Parish is an interesting tale. There exists a charter, dated AD 854 describing the bounds of an estate granted by King Ethelwulf of Wessex to the church of Winchester. Historians refer to this as a spurious charter, in other words the document was probably faked by the monks of Winchester. It is recorded in the Anglo-Saxon Chronicle that shortly before his death Ethelwulf conveyed by charter a tenth of his kingdom to the praise of God and his own eternal salvation. Clearly, he was trying to buy himself a place in heaven. The monks put on their boots and went round Wessex, making up charters to claim valuable bits of land. This charter referred to the area of the later Parish of Hinton and included Earlscourt.[1] Its extent, still traceable today, comprised a long narrow strip of land that extended from the *Smita* (River Cole), its northern boundary, in a south-easterly direction for about 5.75 miles (9.25 kilometres) onto Hinton Downs. At its broadest it was just over a mile (1.6 kilometres) at which point an ancient spring line track – the Icknield Way – passes through West Hinton, then continues through the village of Little Hinton clustered around its church, and onwards passing through Bishopstone village. The parish owes its name, probably acquired by

Fig. 2. Monks walking the boundary of the spurious charter (Nick Boon)

Fig. 3. Saxon sarsen stone boundary marker on Hinton Downs

the tenth century due to the ownership by monks – Hinton in old English means the farm of the (monastic) community.[2] Apparently forming part of a large estate held by the Winchester community at Wanborough in the eleventh century the land had seemingly by the twelfth century acquired a singular identity. By 1066 Earlscourt had become a *lay fee* (dues paid to the secular rather than the religious), and by the twelfth century land, which formed the later Manor of Wanborough, had also passed into lay hands. Thus, the Manor of Hinton, or as it was called from at least the fifteenth century – Little Hinton – alone remained the property of the monks of the Old Minster, Winchester. In 1284 it was confirmed to the Convent of St. Swithun's and in 1300 the Convent received a grant of *free warren* (the right to hunt hares and foxes) there. From at least the fourteenth century the profits of the estate were assigned to the Hoarder of St. Swithun's. The estate passed to the Crown at the Dissolution, but in 1541 was granted to the new cathedral chapter at Winchester, which thereafter held it until the nineteenth century.

Bishopstone

Bishopstone's name translates to farm of the bishops,[3] the bishops being those of Salisbury who are thought to have owned the village as part of their Ramsbury estate. As such Bishopstone's early records were included with those of Ramsbury, and it was not recorded by name until 1208. Unfortunately, being part of the Ramsbury Hundred means that records relating to the settlement are for the early period non-existent and subsequent records are relatively rare. Consequently, little is known regarding Bishopstone's early economic history or the villagers themselves. The Domesday Book records that Ramsbury Hundred had land for 54 ploughs, meadow 80 acres: pasture 14 furlongs long and 5 furlongs wide, woodland 16 furlongs long and 4 furlongs broad. The manorial holding of Ramsbury presents an apparent lack of arable land. Much of its land had been reserved as a hunting park, as early as 1086, for the bishop's hunting and to keep animals for his household use and consumption. The manor of Bishopstone remained in the hands of the bishops until 1647 when it was sold to John Oldfield and Matthew Kendrick.

Paleontology

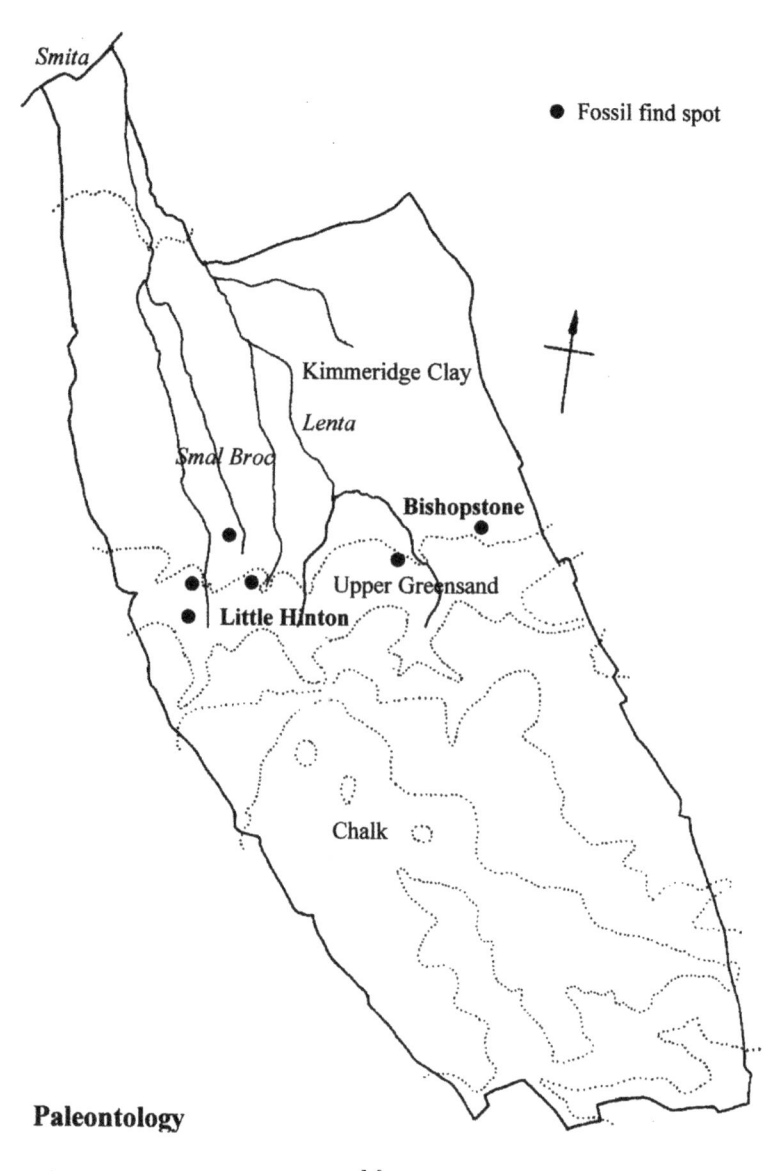

Map 1
The land that is now Bishopstone with Little Hinton Parish during the Late Jurassic and Cretaceous periods (163.5 to 66 million years ago) lay beneath a shallow sea that covered much of northwest Europe. Evidence of this is provided by the discovery of fossilised remains of sea creatures that can be found in the sedimentary geological deposits - Kimmeridge clay to the north, the chalk to the south and in-between the Upper Greensand. Field walking and excavation by the authors have produced fossils disturbed from the Greensand beds that stretch centrally across the parish.

2
Topography and Geology

Passing through the parish, other than the previously mentioned 'Icknield Way' and lying on the down land to the south, is the prehistoric 'Ridgeway' path. A further track known as the 'Rogues Road'[4] extended across the flat clay lands to the north.

Both Bishopstone and Little Hinton village lie at the centre of their former parishes, at the point where the high chalk down lands of the south meets the flat Kimmeridge clay lands to the north. Here springs emerge from coombes cut into the chalk scarp feeding the *Lenta* and *Smal Broc* streams, the waters of which eventually join the River Thames, far to the north. These spring heads have, based on archaeological discoveries, clearly provided a focus for settlement over many millennia.

The area's Ordnance Survey geological maps illustrate that the two villages stand on 'Head' (sediments formed by slope erosion). However, local investigations have demonstrated that beneath them is a terrace of Upper Greensand (a glauconitic fine-grained sandstone) with areas of silty clay.

Evidencing that these geological deposits formed part of an ancient seabed are the occasional find of fossilised remains brought up by the plough or discovered during digging. Found through our field walking and excavation these include fossilised *Ichthyosaur* teeth and bone, as well as clam and oyster shells from the upper greensand and from the flint beds sea urchin. The latter commonly known as shepherds' purse or crown.

Fig. 4. Fossil of a clam of the mid-Cretaceous period, found north of Bishopstone Church

3
British Palaeolithic
(800,000+ to 10,000 years before present)

The words Palaeontology and Palaeolithic are confusingly similar words. Palaeontology means the study of a time before recorded history via fossils and rock structure. Palaeo meaning from a time before recorded history and lithic meaning relating to stone, as in stone tools. As to Mesolithic and Neolithic well... you will just have to carry on reading.

The *Pleistocene* – the final great ice age – is an era that began 2,588,000 years ago and it spans the World's recent period of repeated glaciations when ice sheets up to two miles thick covered much of Europe and North America. The presented image of endless ice is not a true picture, as the era in these regions was punctuated by warm periods when the ice sheets contracted; at least nine major episodes (*interglacials*) and many minors (*interstadials*). Some lasted thousands of years and conditions varied from arctic to warm, and occasionally temperatures were higher than today. Currently we live in the following *Holocene* era which began around 10,000 BC.

The earliest known use of stone tools is around 2.6 million years ago. This heralded the Palaeolithic period which is divided into Lower (245,000 years or more ago), Middle (245,000 to 40,000 years ago) and Upper (40,000 to 10,000 years ago). In Britain, the latter is further divide into three sub-periods: Early Upper, Middle Upper and Later Upper. Connected to Europe and Ireland by land bridges the record of intermittent human occupation during the British Palaeolithic period is divided by episodes when the country was largely or wholly abandoned due to advancing ice sheets. Open tundra dominated by herbs, sedges and grasses with only minimal forest development was grazed by horse, red deer, mammoth, rhino, reindeer, arctic hare, saiga antelope and wild cattle; and was hunted over by brown bear, lynx, hyena, red and arctic fox, and wolf.

The earliest appearance in Britain of humans (*Homo antecessor?*)

was over 800,000 years ago and is evidenced by flint cores, flakes and flake tools discovered on the Norfolk coast near Happisburgh.[5] By 500,000 years ago another group of humans (*Homo heidelbergensis*) had occupied Boxgrove in West Sussex.[6] Archaeological finds there include: a human shin bone and teeth as well as characteristic *Acheulean* oval and pear-shaped flint hand axes and bones of horse, giant deer (*megaloceros*), woolly rhinoceros, vole, and wolf. *Neanderthals* who had intermittently occupied Europe for at least 130,000 years disappeared about 30,000 BC when signs of modern human (*Homo sapiens*) began to appear. Only recently has stratified evidence been found of early *Neanderthal* activity within Britain. Dating to around 100,000 BC the sealed deposit at Dartford in Kent produced struck flint flakes.[7] *Neanderthal* occupation sites dating to 65,000 to 30,000 BC include remains found in a gravel quarry in Norfolk that comprise finely fashioned, elongated D-shape flint axes and the skeletons of several mammoth.

These early inhabitants of Britain were highly mobile, roaming over wide distances hunting migrating animals for food and clothing, and sourcing stone and other materials to make tools. Rough temporary shelters were made from animal skins, wood and bone, or accessible rock shelters and caves were occupied. Besides axes, tools made from stone flakes included spear heads, backed knives, saws, side scrapers and notched flakes. Characteristic of the

Fig. 5. Late Palaeolithic flint scraper/piercer, found north of Little Hinton (length 4.8cm)

Early Upper Palaeolithic period long narrow blades were struck from carefully prepared cores. These were then made into a wide range of tools including leaf-shaped and tanged points, end and nosed scrapers, burins, and piercers. During the Later Upper Palaeolithic the spread and numbers of occupation sites found in Britain increased greatly. Tool making in this period revolved largely around smaller stone implements within which two different technologies are identifiable, Late *Creswellian*

Palaeolithic

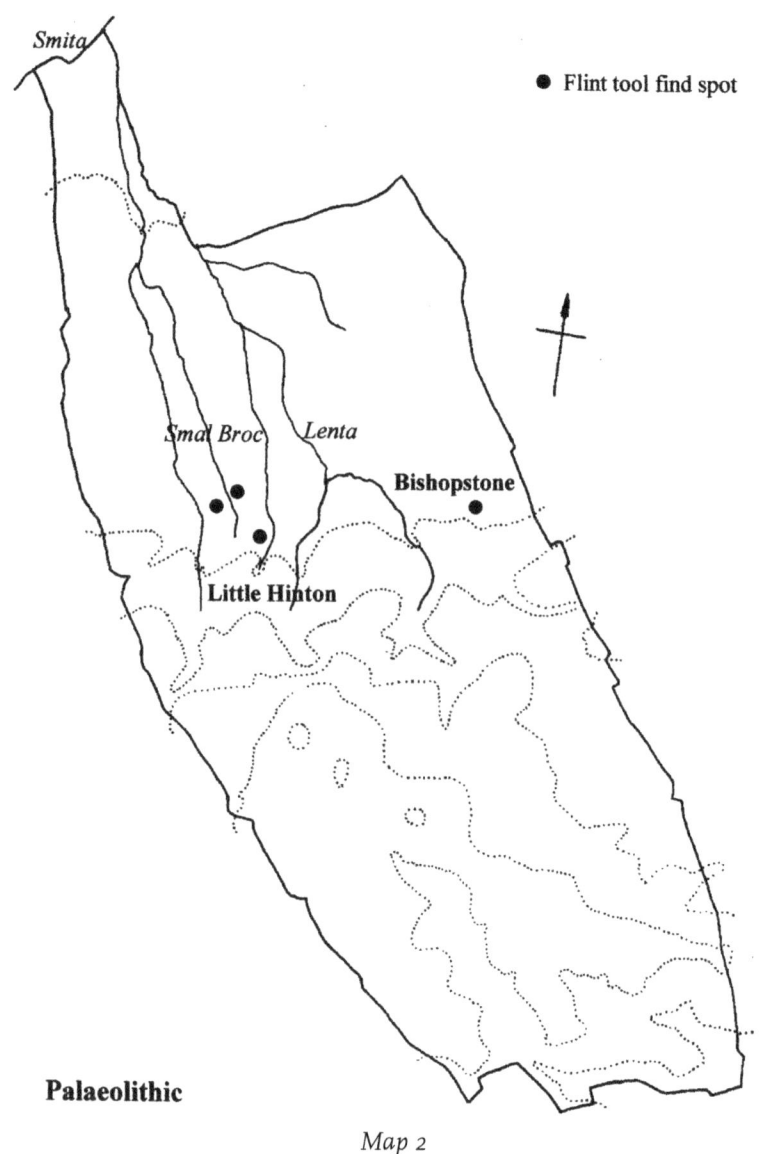

Map 2

The Late Palaeolithic, a time when tundra, created following the retreating ice cap that had covered most of Britain, was undergoing change with the gradual appearance of forests. It is to this period that a few of the flint tools that we have discovered belong. This map shows that their find spots are located close to the area where the northern clay lands give way to the Upper Greensand before the land rises to the chalk downs to the south. It is here that springs issue forth, clearly providing an important focal point for the nomadic people of that time, be it for domestic or ritual functions.

and Final *Creswellian*[8]. Use was also made of bone, antler, shell, amber, animal teeth, mammoth ivory, and wood, which were fashioned into items such as awls, harpoons, needles, and jewellery, as well as rods thought to be batons, symbols of authority. Artistic expression seems to have been limited although a remarkable engraving of a horse on a rib bone and cave art at Creswell Crags[9] and the Mendip caves are notable exceptions.

About 11,800 years ago as the climate became cooler and drier, woodland began to appear, as revealed by birch and willow pollen samples. As a result, the traditional types of animal hunted declined, bringing about a need to adapt flint-knapping techniques to produce new tool types that enabled the hunting of the different incoming animal species.

Palaeolithic Activity Evidence
Evidence relating to this period, within the Parish, is confined to a few flint tools that derive from the Upper Palaeolithic era (41,000 to 10,000 years ago). A trench cut through a paddock near Little Hinton Manor[10] produced a struck flake having a notch on one corner and a retouched cutting edge. Nearby, from ploughed fields to the north came a core that had been used as a hammer stone and then re-worked to provide a cutting or scraping edge, and a combined drill and scraper, whilst from plough soil, east of Bishopstone, came an end scraper.

4
Mesolithic
(8,000 BC – 4,000 BC)

We call this period the Mesolithic, which hardly needs interpretation, easy to guess that meso means middle. We have reached the Middle Stone Age. Glaciers melting, due to the higher temperatures, resulted in rising sea levels so that Britain became separated from Ireland and later from Europe (a story that seems to repeat, were they also worried about climate change?).

Around 8,000 BC with temperatures rising to those like today, the tundra and lightly wooded landscape gradually turned to thick deciduous forests that stretched from one end of Britain to the other. Composed of birch, hazel, oak, elm, lime, and alder, and interspersed with pine, the forests were only broken by river and stream courses, lakes, marshland, and mountain tops. These wildwoods were inhabited by red and roe deer, *aurochs* (wild cattle), boar, wild pig, elk, beaver, wolf, wild cat, brown bear, otter and pine marten, along with a variety of bird life. Glaciers melting due to the higher temperatures resulted in escalating sea levels so that Britain became separated from Ireland around 9,500 years ago and about 1,000 years later from Europe.

Hunter Gathers

Groups of hunters and gatherers would have been small, perhaps no more than thirty of all ages and confined most likely to kinship or intimate union. A Mesolithic cemetery excavated in Skateholm, Sweden,[11] included burials accompanied with dogs. Seemingly they had become domesticated due to their hunting abilities amongst reeds and dense undergrowth. Stone tools developed to accommodate new hunting techniques needed within the forest and wetland environments. Tiny microliths were formed from small bladelets struck from flint cores using punches and hammers of antler, bone, or wood. Combined, these tiny flints set into wood and secured by resin and fibre created harpoons, barbed arrows, reaping hooks and grating blocks.[12] Most tool types of

- Flint tool find spot
- Flint tools find spot

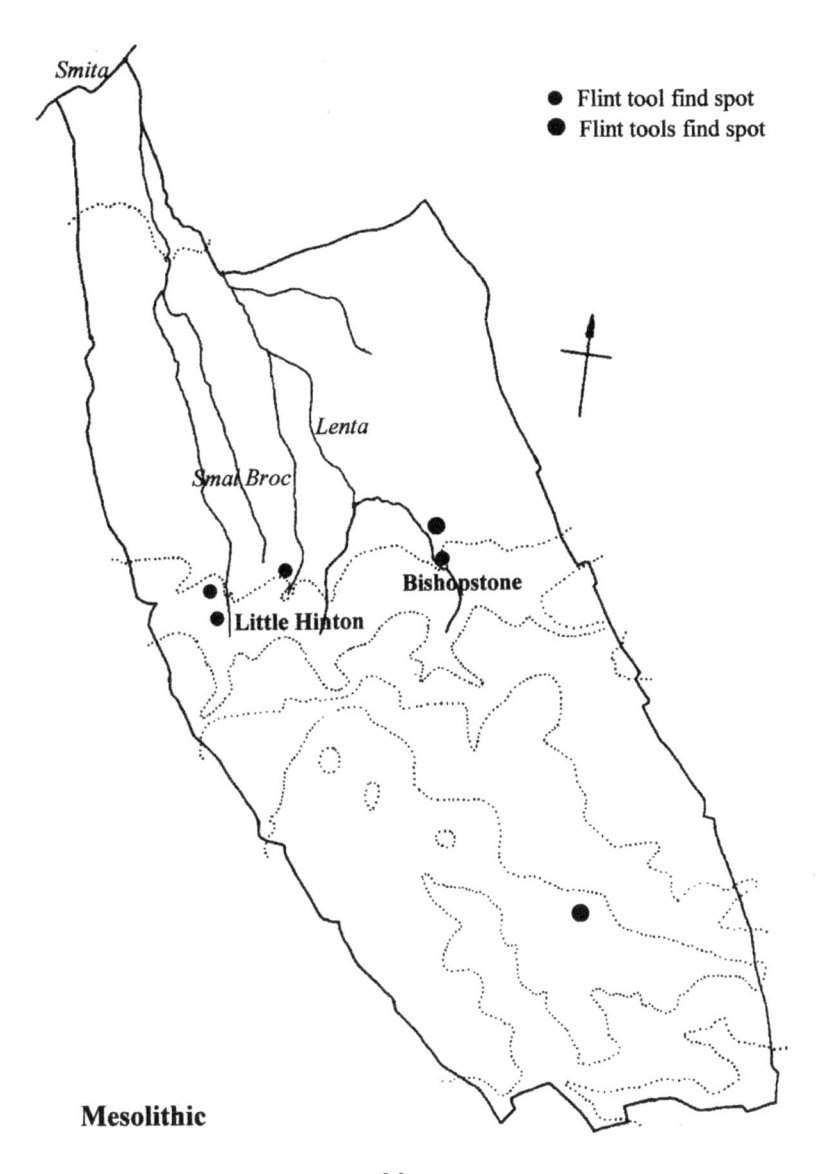

Mesolithic

Map 3
Now, in the Mesolithic era, the forests - the wildwood - stretched from one end of Britain to the other. Within the forests the small groups of nomadic people set up semi-permanent or temporary camps. The location of the flint tools of this period that we and others have discovered, again demonstrate the importance of the springs. However, on the edge of the southern chalk downs, overlooking the lands to the north, an isolated camp site is evidenced, perhaps a base for hunting from or gathering flint for making tools.

Fig. 6. Mesolithic flints from Russley Downs

the Upper Palaeolithic continued to be made, but two large implements appeared – the pick for digging and the adze for woodworking. Recent archaeological discoveries have shown that Mesolithic people were not, as previously considered, entirely nomadic as besides overnight or seasonal encampments they occupied long term residential bases with substantial timber-framed circular buildings. Each site may have been re-visited regularly over a considerable time span. The seasonal camps were probably linked to specific requirements sourced at relevant periods of the year that may have included access to manufacturing materials, various food types and traditional or spiritual events.

Specific site activities are seemingly demonstrated through the range and number of tools found. Small, concentrated groups with a majority of microliths hint at temporary foraging/hunting camps, while a wide variety of tools spread over an extensive area indicate a semi-permanent occupation.

Mesolithic Activity Evidence

At present activity during this period is, like the earlier period, slight being confined to a small quantity of struck flints. The densest concentration consists of a scraper, a core, a saw blade, and a notched blade along with numerous flakes from a ploughed field on Russley Downs. At the mill in Bishopstone an archaeological test pit produced a scraper from a silt deposit of recent date, suggesting that the flint tool had been washed downstream from the coombe that lies south of the village. Close to at Cue's Lane excavation in advance of building work produced a number of struck flints. A few flints of the period were also found close to Little Hinton: a snapped blade southeast of Little Hinton village hall, a knife blade east of the Grove and a hollow scraper from Holy Well.

5
Neolithic
(4,000 BC – 2,600 BC)

And then the New Stone Age came along when we decided to grow up and start working for our living. Those modern ideas crept in from abroad. Why chase your food and forage when you can clear the land and grow stuff next to the permanent dwelling that you have constructed, and catch animals and keep them close? Of course, perhaps it took a while to realise that all this land clearing and stock rearing would take up all your time when you were not making those new-fangled clay pots or baking bread. Whoever invented bread anyway? Talking of which, one also had to discover new gods and goddesses, the sort that would help control the seasons and make it rain or not, depending on what one needed at that moment. So, when you roll over and groan as the alarm wakes you at 6.30am – oh joy! Another day on the treadmill – you know who to blame.

An improving warm climate saw a reduction of pine and an increase of deciduous woodland. Within it an increasing population, and consequently a shortage of hunting and gathering resources heralded the need for alternate methods of obtaining food. Farming techniques introduced from the continent made an appearance in Britain around 4,100 BC, firstly in the Greater Thames Estuary then gradually spreading to other parts and reaching the Upper Thames Valley around 3,900 BC.[13] As a result, woodland was rapidly cleared to provide arable land for the growing of barley and emmer wheat, and pasture for domesticated herds of cattle and pig. Recent archaeological work has shown that within the clearings substantial post-built rectangular houses were erected. Surrounding woodland continued to be foraged for timber and food such as hazel nuts, edible roots, berries, fungi, tubers, and crab apples. Settlement became more permanent, moving only being a necessity when cleared land became unproductive or resources in the neighbouring woodland were exhausted.

Fig. 7. An earthen long barrow on the Wanborough/Liddington parish boundary (centre of the picture)

Distinct tribal territories appear to have been established, marked by earthen monuments, which were ditched enclosures that defined special places for ritual, trading, or multi-tribal gatherings as well as earthen burial mounds being places of transformation, a connection between the living, the spirit world and mother earth. A hierarchy and priesthood now clearly existed which could organise the manpower needed for monument construction. Such structures evoked a sense of belonging, identity, veneration for the dead and spiritual belief. Other major changes are apparent, notably the making of pottery vessels, leaf shaped flint arrowheads, flint mining and the polishing of stone axes to turn them into desirable symbols of wealth and power.

Neolithic Settlement Evidence
This period is chiefly represented within the parish by struck flints, but also includes a few fragments of pottery vessels. It is additionally a period when former structural evidence is first presented.

- 1-5 Flint tool find spot
- 5 + Flint tools find spot
* Long barrow (site of)
P Pottery

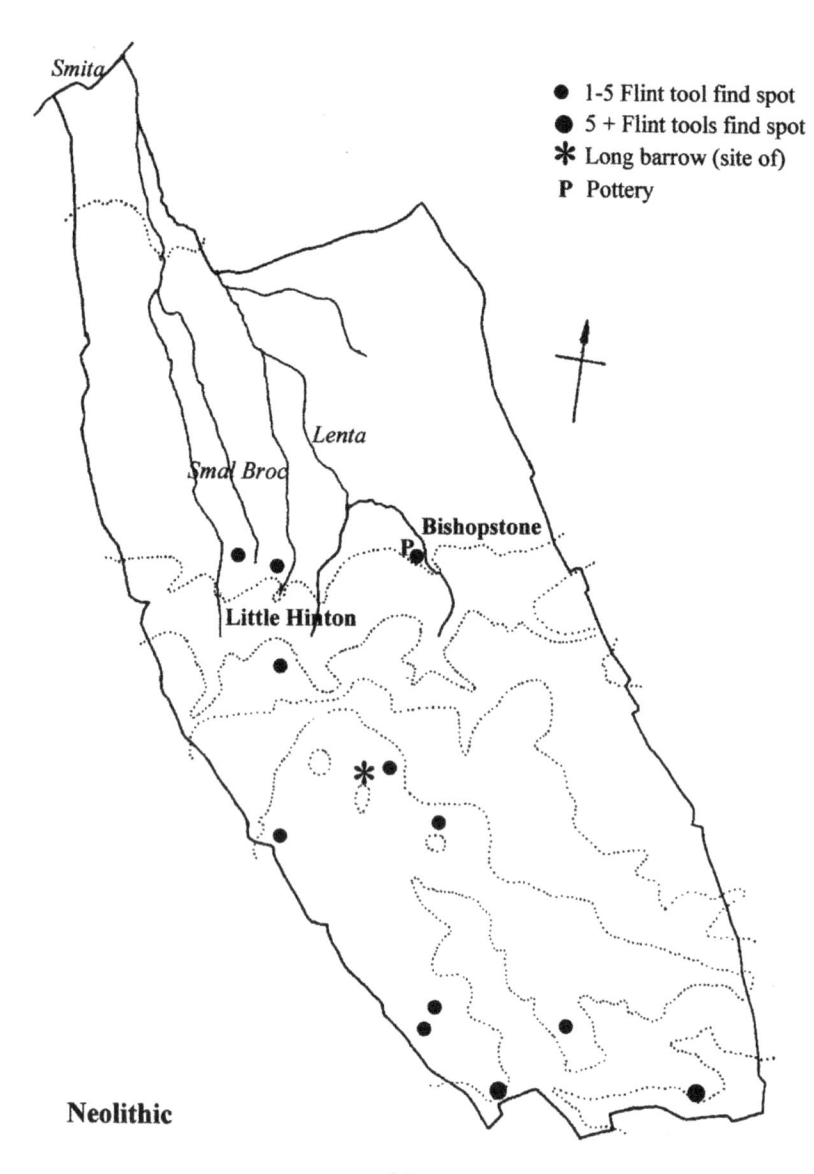

Neolithic

Map 4
The Neolithic era saw much of the Wild Wood that covered the chalk cut down exposing its lighter topsoil, so making land available for permanent dwellings, and areas for planting crops and raising animals. Whilst we and others have found flint tools and the occasional pottery sherd around the springs and over the high chalk downs to the south, there is a total lack of such finds from the clay lands to the north, suggesting that, due to the heavier soils, the woodland remained intact.

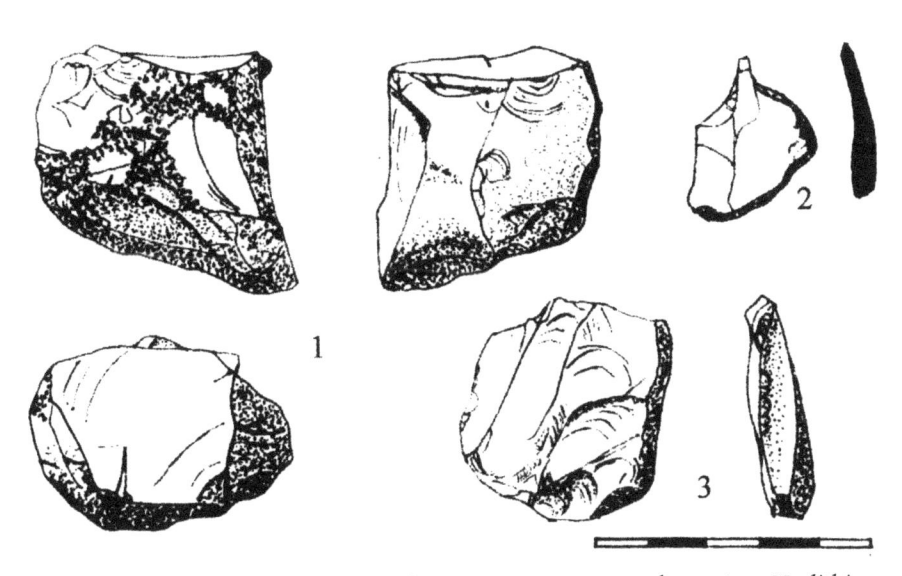

Fig. 8. Prehistoric struck flint tools from Hinton Manor (scale 5cm) 1. Neolithic flake core having secondary use as a hammer stone. 2. Neolithic piercer. 3. Upper Palaeolithic side scraper

East of Charlbury Hill records held in Salisbury Museum indicate that a long barrow (burial mound) existed but was destroyed in 1870. Its earthen mound was said to be 135 feet long by 30 feet wide (41.1m x 9.1m), and three skulls were noted by a Mr F Sidford. A similar barrow, although severely damaged exists in the adjacent Wanborough Parish at Wanborough Warren. From that mound protrude sarsen stones evidencing a burial chamber. An extensive settlement site is evidenced at the southern end of the parish, within a valley bottom near Gore Farm. Here a scatter of struck flints including scrapers, a borer, blades, a hammer stone, a core, and many flakes were recovered from plough soil. Another such site is indicated by the finding of a core, a discoidal knife, two fabricators, a flake worked to create a knife and a flake at Foxhill. Other chance finds of struck flints comprise: a fragment of a greenstone polished axe-head; a core reused as a hammer stone and two circular scrapers on Hinton Downs, and a polished axe from near Charlbury Hill. Also found were an end and side scraper, two hammer stones, and a notched flake from City Corner, Little Hinton; a flint end scraper and small blade from west of White Hill; and a flint core and a piercer found during an excavation at Hinton Manor. Pottery sherds came from a trial excavation[14] undertaken by the authors north of Bishopstone Church. One sherd, decorated with multiple stab marks, probably came from a bowl of so-called Mortlake type and dates to around 3,200 BC.

Fig. 9. Neolithic polished flint axe head from near Charlbury Hill

6
Bronze Age
(2,600-700 BC)

It was found by heating up certain rocks people could extract this strange molten material that as it cooled got extremely hard, they called it metal (in their own language, of course). Copper had been known about since the extremely late Neolithic, but now there were other sorts of metal, gold, tin, and lead. Because some idiot could not leave well alone, they started smelting and mixing metals. Copper and tin together formed an alloy – bronze – not only was it attractively shiny and hard, when the molten bronze was poured into moulds, say axe shaped, it would make a tool or weapon (now we have land to fight over). So, the old flint tools began to go out of use.

Fig. 10. Bronze Age bowl barrow on Hinton Downs

Recent DNA evidence strongly points to incoming people from across the English Channel who in a short period of time wiped out the indigenous Neolithic population. These newcomers have been given the name 'Beaker People' due to the highly decorated vessels found in their graves. Around 2,150 BC metalworkers discovered that by adding a small amount of tin to copper a much harder material – bronze – was obtained. This enabled the manufacture of a greater range of weapons and tools that included axes, daggers, awls, gouges, and scythes. Flint

- Artefact find spot
P Pottery find spot
* Bowl barrow
■ Settlement site
○ Ring ditch

Smita
Lenta
Smal Broc
Bishopstone
Little Hinton
Ridgeway

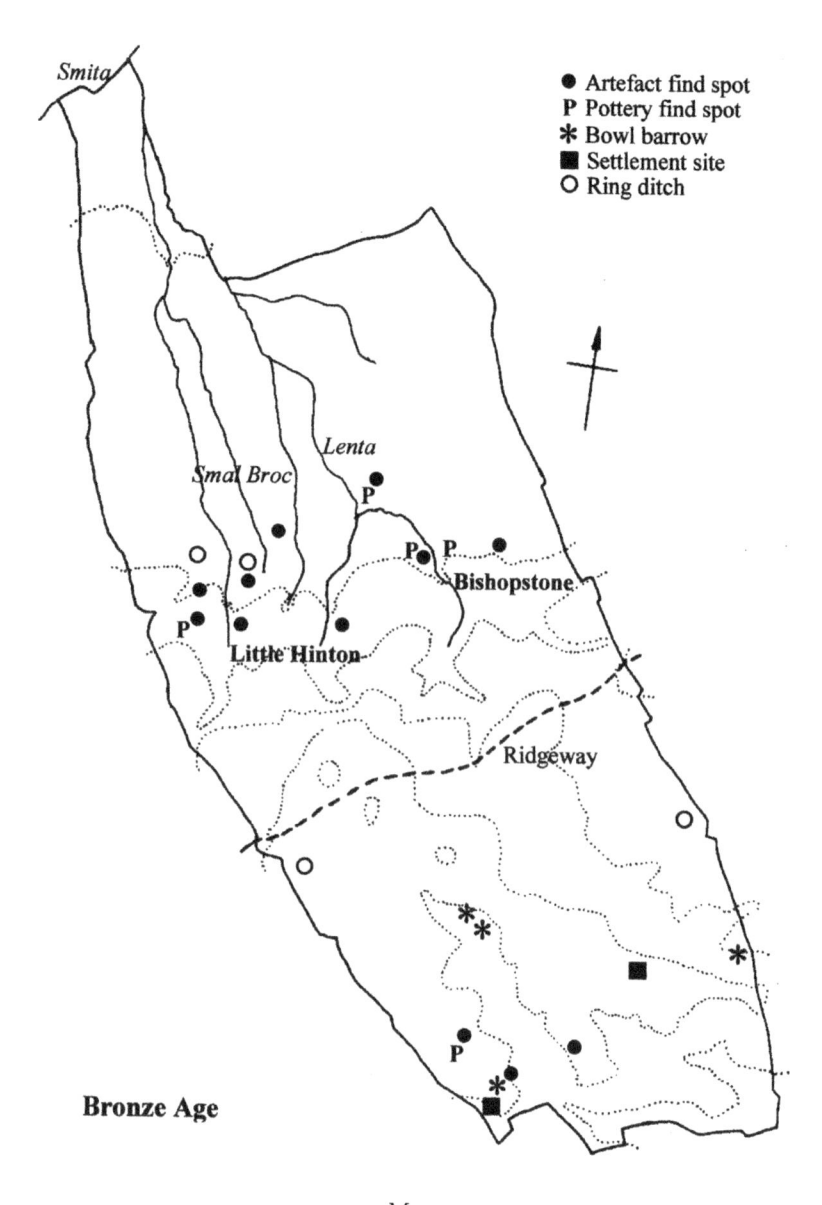

Bronze Age

Map 5
The Bronze Age saw people establishing permanent settlements within a checkerboard pattern of fields, bounded by the burial mounds of their dead. Once more the distribution of flint tools and pottery we and others have found, along with surviving burial mounds, demonstrate that the spring-line was still an important location in the landscape along with the southern chalk land. There also appears to be some encroachment onto the clay lands to the north.

Fig. 11. Bronze dagger from Old Town, Swindon (length 11.5cms)

though, continued to be used for the making of scrapers, awls, knives and arrowheads. Also, a wider range of pottery vessel types were now made – beaker, urn, food vessel, cup, storage and serving pot. Clothes were produced in leather, wool and possibly linen. This period saw the creation of long-lasting settlements, since food supplies were assured through the efficient cultivation of cereals and the husbandry of animals. Settlements though were small, and the circular houses built were of slight construction. A wealthy hierarchy is indicated using gold as jewellery and ornamentation. Additionally, and perhaps indicating the need to defend territory and position bronze weapons for warfare – rapiers, swords, and spears – were now used.

Late Bronze Age

Commencing around 1,200 BC the Late Bronze Age saw the erection of substantial roundhouses in bigger enclosed settlements with clearly defined fields and circular burial mounds erected on land borders, so demonstrating concepts of domesticity, identity, and property rights. Fields were small and rectangular and can be seen preserved as cropmarks or earthworks on the chalk downs. Divided by trackways, enclosures, and settlement areas they formed a patchwork that covered substantial areas. Further evidencing territorial boundaries and a desire to

Fig. 12. City Corner, Little Hinton ring ditch excavation

increase control over wide-ranging land are the arrival of long ditches, some many miles in length, often associated with fortified hilltop enclosures.

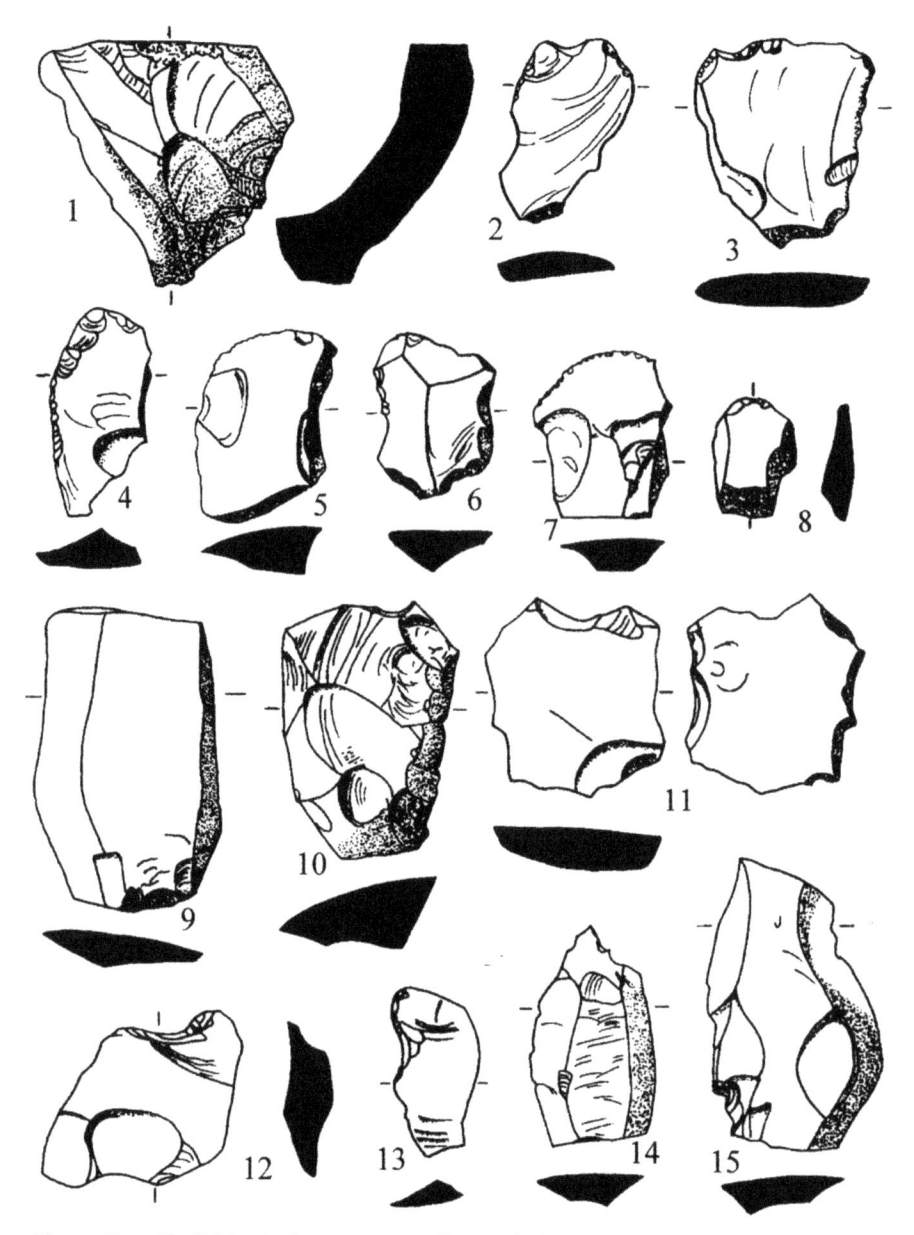

Fig. 13. Late Neolithic/Early Bronze Age flint tools from North of Bishopstone Church (fig 13.9 length 5.2cms)

1. Core having two striking platforms.
2. Flake with a shallow notch on the distal end, and a second notch on an adjoining edge, along with an area of semi-abrupt retouch.
3. Flake having at its distal end a small notch.
4. Blade having an area of abrupt retouch on one side and intrusive retouch at the tip.
5. Flake having a curved serrated cutting edge. Both adjacent sides have been struck to provide thumb and index finger holds.
6. Flake with, at the proximal end, a scraping edge formed by abrupt retouch, at the distal end a small point formed by retouch and on one side a broad notch.
7. Flake having a rounded serrated cutting edge. Both adjacent sides have been struck to provide thumb and index finger holds.
8. Small flake having at the distal end, and one side, retouch forming scraping edges.
9. Broad, knife blade.
10. Blade with a notch at the distal end.
11. Flake having at the proximal end a scraping edge, at the distal end a small point and on one side a broad notch.
12. Flake notched at the distal end with on the opposing edge a single, invasive strike creating a firm thumb hold.
13. Blade with a notch and retouch on one edge.
14. Blade with a roughly formed point at the distal end.
15. Broad, knife blade

Bronze Age Settlement Evidence

Within the parish, besides struck flints, pottery, and a few bronze artefacts the Bronze Age period is evidenced by several extant round barrows. These earthen tombs, usually built over a single burial, took a variety of forms the commonest being the bowl barrow, which comprised a hemispherical mound of earth surrounded by a ditch. Four such barrows have been identified within the Parish of which three have been investigated by antiquarians. One on Hinton Downs, opened in 1889, contained a cremation in an oval grave with a bronze dagger. Two, lying close together in a valley bottom north of Downs Barn, were excavated around 1922 and found to contain cremations. A fourth barrow was located west of Harley Bushes in 1934. Levelled by ploughing other barrows have been revealed by their ditches showing as circular marks in growing crops. One such barrow at City Corner in Little Hinton measures around 20m in diameter. Its ring ditch was investigated by the authors via a small trial trench which showed the ditch to be 0.8m deep, around 3m wide and to have a dished profile.

Before the excavation, a Bronze Age flint fabricator had been found in the overlying plough soil. Other circular barrow ditches have been noted on: Lammy Down; Hinton Downs; northeast of Starveall Farm and north of the Grove near Little Hinton. Evidence of settlement sites are more elusive. An excavation in advance of building work at Cues Lane, Bishopstone[15] produced sixty pottery fragments and a trial excavation by the authors,[16] on the opposite side of the *Lenta* stream, found further sherds and many struck flint tools and flakes. A spread of pottery sherds and a flint thumb scraper found on Hinton Downs close to a bowl barrow, and a scatter of pottery fragments north of Russley Park most likely indicate other settlement sites. Amongst casual finds of note are a fragments of a bronze scabbard chape, a small bronze terret and a small bronze figurine in the form of a sheep found on Hinton Downs.

7
Iron Age
(700BC to AD43)

Ah yes, the Iron Age, as archaeologists think of it, but this is also called, more romantically, as the age of the Celts. I met a young person at Avebury who told me that she was a reincarnation of a Celt. When I told her that if it were so she would certainly not have claimed to be a Celt, since Celt or Keltoi was the derogatory term used by the Greeks and Romans for the barbaric tribes of northern Europe, she was a little put out.

Although introduced into Britain from southern Europe around 750 BC iron working technology that marked the beginning of the Iron Age was not commonly employed until around 500 BC. Iron ore though was plentiful in Britain and easily obtainable. The resulting metal being much stronger than bronze revolutionised many aspects of daily life particularly iron tipped ploughs that could turn up even clay soils quicker and deeper than those of wood, or those tipped with bronze.

Fig. 14. Liddington Castle, Iron Age hill fort

Woodland could be cleared faster with iron axes enabling much more farmland to be created for an ever-growing population.

Settlement and Agriculture
Ruled by chieftains, the population lived mainly within substantial circular huts on isolated farms spread across the tribal territory. Around these, the inhabitants in the Early Iron Age grew crops and raised animals.

Fig. 15. Model of an Iron Age hut (Swindon Museum)

According to the fourth century BC Greek geographer and voyager Pytheas, Iron Age Britons were famed wheat farmers. This is clearly shown in the preserved flora and fauna remains found which includes spelt and emmer wheat, barley, rye, and oats. Cattle were a source of portable wealth, as well as providing useful domestic by-products like milk, cheese, beef, and leather. In the later Iron Age, it appears that cattle, however, ceased to be the main animal reared giving way to the less labour-intensive rearing of sheep, which besides mutton provided wool for cloth making. Pig, horse, dog and less commonly chicken are also widely represented in the osteo-archaeological record.

Pressure on land available for cultivation invariably resulted in warfare between adjoining tribes over boundaries. This undoubtedly was the chief reason for construction throughout the Early Iron Age and into the Middle Iron Age of fortified enclosures and hillforts, some of which were on a massive scale. The latter would have served as centres where tribal groups could retreat in times of threat as well as a place for tribal gatherings, trading, and religious activities. However, in about 350 BC they largely went out of use. Those remaining in use though were substantially reinforced, perhaps indicating the merger of existing tribes into larger and consequently stronger groups.

The first British coinage in gold and silver appeared in Southern Britain around 150 BC and later bronze coins were struck. Designs were

ITS ARCHAEOLOGY AND HISTORY 27

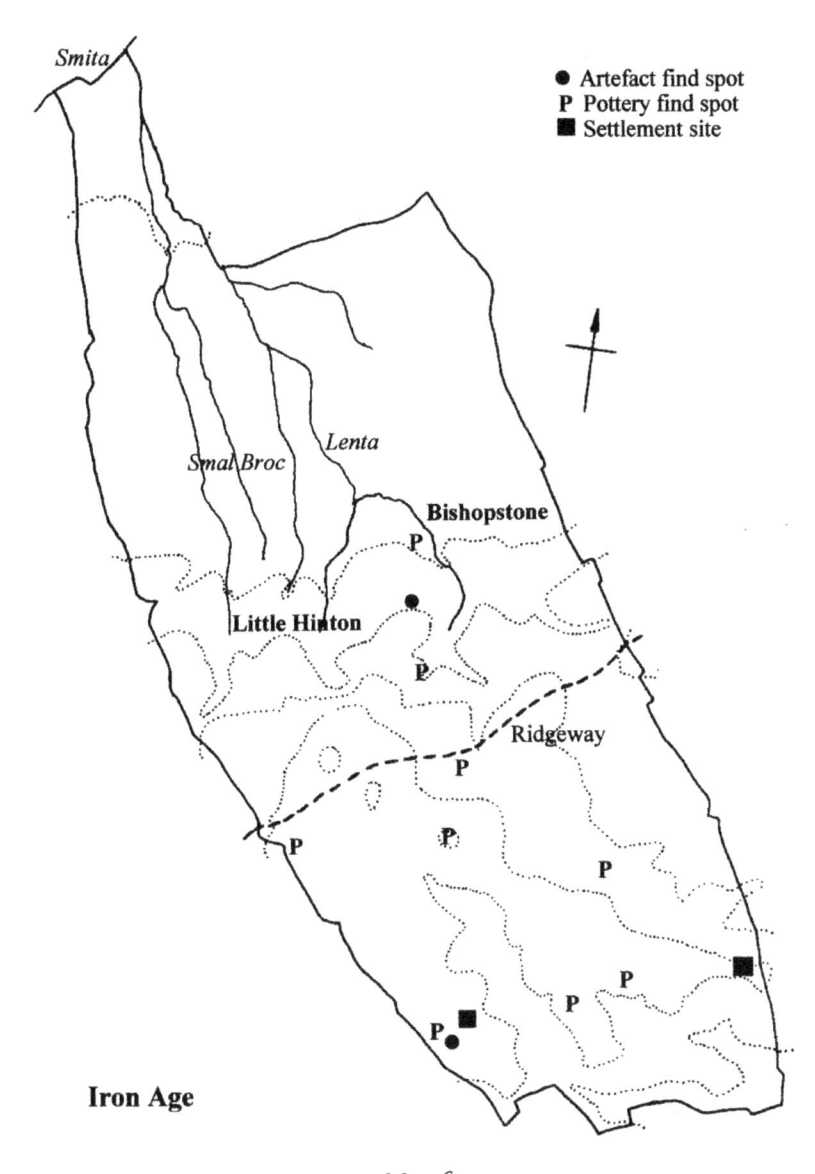

Iron Age

Map 6
A track, the Ridgeway, link the nearby Iron Age hillforts of Liddington Castle and Uffington Castle. This ancient track lies central to the Parish lands. During the Iron Age the spring-line, to the north of the track, seems to have lost its appeal with only a few finds from near Bishopstone village. Our finds from field walking, and those found by others, show that activity was confined to the distant southern chalk land, notably two settlement areas on Russley Downs and Hinton Downs.

Fig. 16. Gold Stater of the East Wiltshire Tribe

initially based on continental coin types bearing stylised horses and disjointed heads. Some of the later examples bore the names of tribal leaders and displayed a diversity of figures, animals, and motifs.

Based on the distribution of coins recent research shows that the area within which the Parish lies was a territory ruled by an Iron Age tribe whose name is unknown. Designated the 'East Wiltshire' tribe it appears to have held an area that stretched from the River Thames to a little south of the River Kennet.[17] It is thought that their tribal centre lay southeast of Marlborough at Forest Hill on the edge of Savernake Forest and that their civitas capital in the Roman period was *Cvnetio* (Mildenhall near Marlborough). To the south were the *Atrebates*, to the east the *Catuvellauni* and another unknown tribe who, seemingly, was eventually annexed by the *Atrebates*. The East Wiltshire tribe's distinctive gold and silver coinage minted for a short period (50-35 BC) was influenced by coins of the *Dobunnic* and *Atrebatic* tribes. The coins depict horses, solar spirals and solar wheels.[18] It would seem from the lack of later coins that they were annexed by a larger tribe, probably the *Dobunni* who bordered to the north and west.

Religion and Death

Various religious practices revolved around offerings and sacrifices which were sometimes human but more often involved the ritual

Fig. 17. Fragment of decorated bone weaving comb from Russley Downs

slaughter of animals or the deposition of metalwork below ground or in water. Also disused storage pits and the terminals of ditches occasionally produce deliberate offerings. These ritual events would have been largely carried out or overseen by an order of priests known as druids. A few buildings used for spiritual purposes have been located within hillforts and as separate complexes identifiable largely by offerings, location, and ground plan. However, religious ceremony could have been undertaken in sacred groves which would have left little evidence for archaeologists to find.

No hillfort exists within the parish, but the Ridgeway, extending through it, links the nearest – Liddington Castle and Uffington Castle.

Iron Age Settlement Evidence
A substantial settlement on Bishopstone Downs is indicated by the discovery, following ploughing, of pottery sherds, a bone weaving comb, a large stone rubber and blackened earth. Probably from this site four bronze brooches, an iron ring-headed pin and a bead-rim pot are stated as being found near Russley Park many years ago. Pottery fragments, brooches, an iron spearhead, worked bone and a gold quarter stater point to a similar settlement on Hinton Downs. Amongst isolated finds are an iron socketed and looped axe-head and a bronze mount in the form of a schematised mask with curved horns and a split flowing beard.

8
Romano-British
(AD 43-450)

Bah! What have the Romans done for us? Their legions and administrators introducing a new way of life. We, the Iron Age people, got on well without their so-called civilisation, who needs straight paved roads? And as for bath houses, we managed quite well with a dip in the local stream once a year. We do not need underfloor heating, that is just for softies. And what about those big stone buildings? You cannot beat good old timber and thatch.

Archaeological evidence for this period is prolific and densely spread, signifying that during the four hundred years of Roman rule substantial population growth and prosperity occurred through successful government and military control.

It began in AD 43 with the invasion decreed by Claudius to secure his position as emperor and gain prestige. The eventual aim was to use the country's wealth in land, labour, and resources to enrich the Roman state and help support its massive military machine. General Plautius landed, probably at Richborough in Kent, at the head of 40,000 troops with all the necessary equipment, transport, food etc. to keep them supplied during the initial stages of the campaign. They landed without opposition but shortly after fought a two-day battle at a crossing on the River Medway. The main field army of the *Catevaulauni*, the leading force in southeast Britain was destroyed. Then the legions pressed northward and captured the *Catevaulauni Oppidum* (fortified settlement) at Colchester (*Camulodunum*). During this early stage of the invasion, it is recorded that eleven tribal kings offered their allegiance to Rome, including the *Dobunni* tribe whose territory, seemingly, incorporated the area in which the Bishopstone with Little Hinton Parish lies. The army then split into several groups; the *Legio II* commanded by Vespasian, a future emperor, headed into the southwest. In opposition to the advancing troops, the local population took refuge in hillforts. According to the Roman writer Suetonius, Vespasian's troops fought thirty battles,

ITS ARCHAEOLOGY AND HISTORY 31

Romano-British

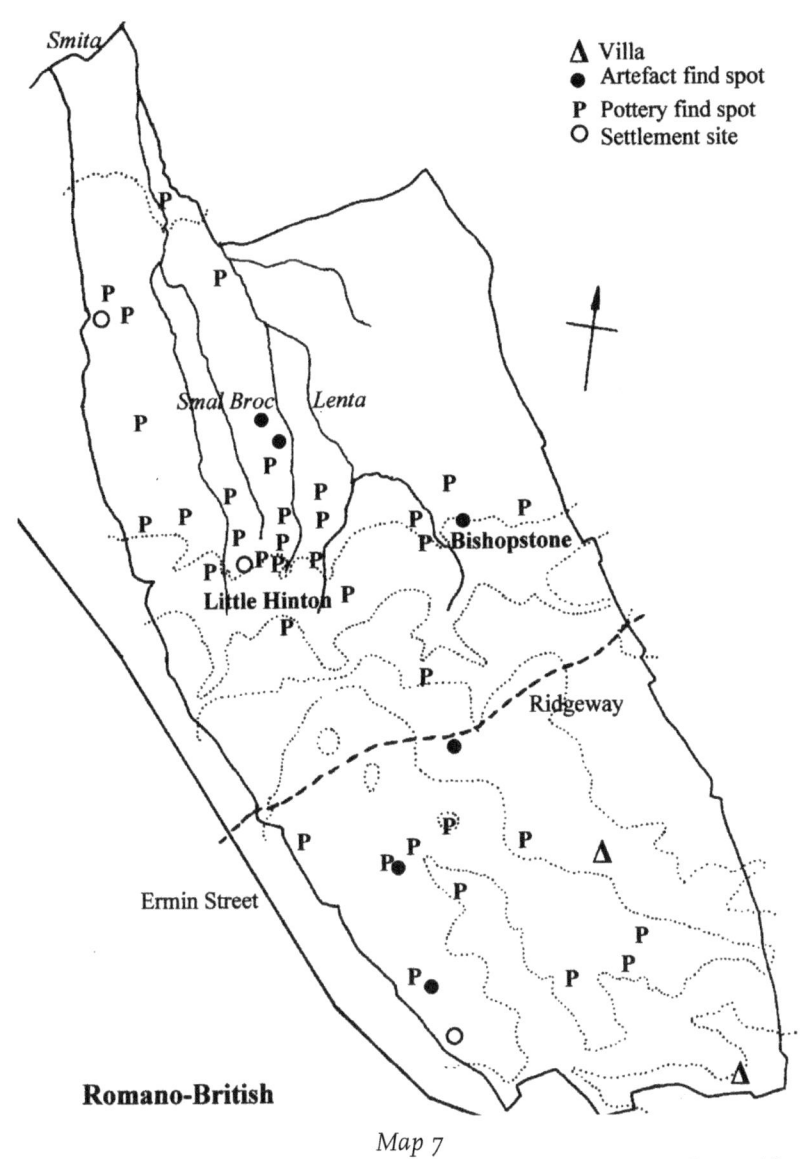

Map 7

As the map shows, during the Romano-British period activity in the parish was extensive. Finds made by us and others show that activity had returned to the spring line as well as onto the northern clay lands with likely building sites at Mount Pleasant, Little Hinton and Bishopstone. On the southern chalk downs two villa sites are located - Starveall Farm and Russley Park - whilst a farmstead site is hinted at on Hinton Downs. Surrounding these sites spreads of worn pottery sherds point to cultivation, the sherds being derived from amongst stockyard and domestic waste collected for spreading as fertilizer on the fields.

overcame two powerful tribes, captured the Isle of Wight, and took over twenty hillforts. His force had apparently started out from a supply base in the Fishbourne or Chichester area and advanced overland against the *Durotriges*, the western *Atrebates* and the tribes of Devon and Cornwall. Meanwhile the navy sailed westward taking the Isle of Wight (*Vectis*) and it established supply bases along the south coast. As the legions progressed, they built supply roads and constructed forts at road junctions and river crossings. One such road, *Ermin Street*, the Roman road from *Calleva Atrebatum* (Silchester) to *Glevum* (Gloucester), lies just outside the Parish's western border. On it at a major road junction not far from the Parish's north-western boundary a Roman town developed, seemingly initially associated with a military establishment, as evidenced by early coins, pottery, and weapons[19]. This town at Lower Wanborough, identified as *Durocornovium* from a late second or early third century AD road map, which gave routes with mileage throughout the Roman Empire, would have served as an administration centre and market for the surrounding rural settlements. Also, a *mansio*, a wayside

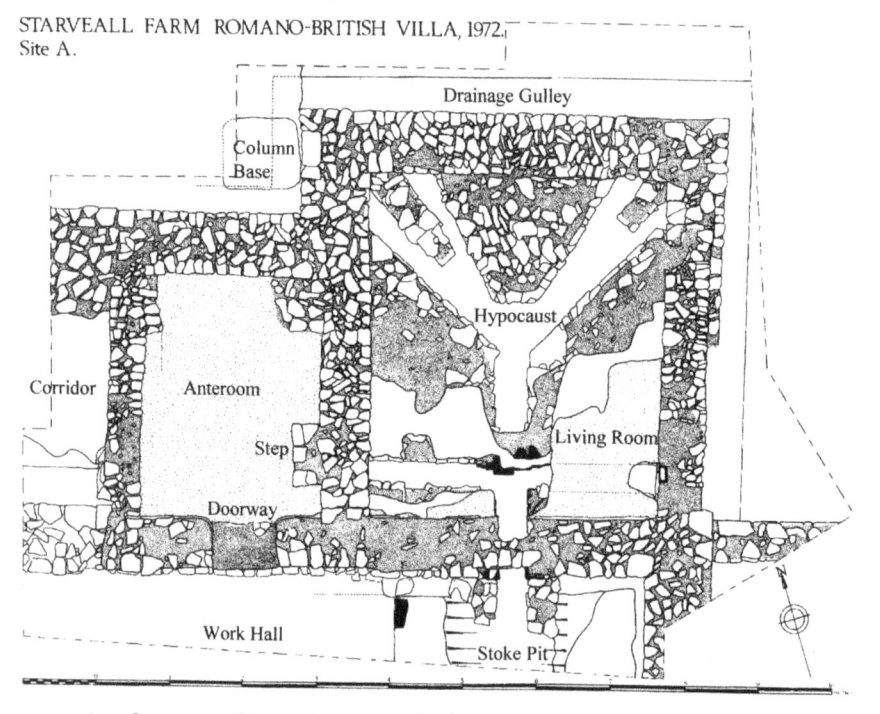

Fig. 18. Starveall Farm Roman Villa house excavation 1972 (scale 11m)

post-house for military and governmental officials, has been identified there[20]. In the later Roman period, the town lay on the eastern boundary of a province known as *Britannia Prima*.

Roman Settlement Evidence

Settlements within the parish ranged from small homesteads to grand villas. One such villa has been identified near Starveall Farm through chance discoveries during cultivation, aerial photography, geo-physics, and excavation[21]. Here the villa buildings are set within a ditched enclosure. Two of the buildings have been partially examined by archaeological excavation, the location of four others have been identified through surface debris observed following ploughing. Two rooms, part

Fig. 19. Surviving mosaic flooring at Starveal Farm Villa

of a corridor and a little of an inner work hall, were revealed of the chalk walled, villa house in 1972. One of the rooms, the easternmost and larger, had a hypocaust with its stoking area situated within the work hall to the rear. This heated room, like the adjacent unheated room, had traces of mosaic flooring surviving. The early fourth century AD mosaic in the larger room had been largely destroyed in antiquity in the search, presumably,

Fig. 20. Mosaic fragment depicting a hound from Starveal Farm Villa (scale 4cms)

for building material and in subsequent ploughing. From the hypocaust's infill however came pieces of the mosaic's central panel. These depict parts of a hunting dog, a tree, and a cloaked figure, which is thought to represent the mythological character Acteon. Acteon, who was trained in the art of hunting, fell foul of the goddess Artemis who, in anger, turned him into a stag and thus he was killed by his hunting hounds. Such a floor design warns of the perils of offending the gods. Also found were pieces of wall plaster painted in purple, yellow, red, white, grey, and blue revealing how vibrantly the room, a dining/reception room, was decorated. Other finds include second to fourth century AD pottery and a bronze brooch.

To the northwest a possible rectangular building, located by geophysical survey, was confirmed by digging a small trench. It was found to have mortared chalk and flint block walling and a carved sandstone slab threshold in a doorway. At some stage, this entrance had been deliberately blocked.

Fig. 21. Painted wall plaster from Starveall Farm Villa (scale 4cms)

A second villa site has been located east of Russley Park. Following ploughing chalk walling was revealed and from the surrounding soil came: first to fourth century pottery sherds; iron nails; animal bones; oolitic limestone roofing tiles; terracotta flue tiles; and a quern stone. Aerial photographs taken of marks in the plough soil show that the villa buildings lie within an enclosure which is bounded by an extensive field system. Just across the adjacent County border cropmarks revealed an enclosure. Subsequent field walking of this produced many quern stone fragments, roofing tiles and iron slag that suggests it was the villa's work compound.

On Hinton Downs another settlement site, most likely a farmstead, has been identified through many finds. Included are coins, first to fourth century AD pottery fragments, and bronze brooches.

A late first/second century AD Roman building site is apparent at City Corner, Little Hinton, evidenced by numerous pottery sherds. Examination of an adjacent hedgerow revealed further sherds, some quite large, and many big sarsen stones, presumably derived from field clearance and originating from ploughed-out building foundations. A trench cut for a drainage pipe in an adjacent grassed field at 'Holywell', a spring site, produced many Roman pottery fragments of a similar date, as well as animal bone. A small trial trench cut by the authors on the line of the pipe trench revealed that the pottery came from the silting of an extensive former pond, at least 1.5m deep, which originally the spring must have fed into. Adjacent slight earthworks may point to the location of an associated building.

Fig. 22. Holywell, Little Hinton, location of an ancient medicinal spring?

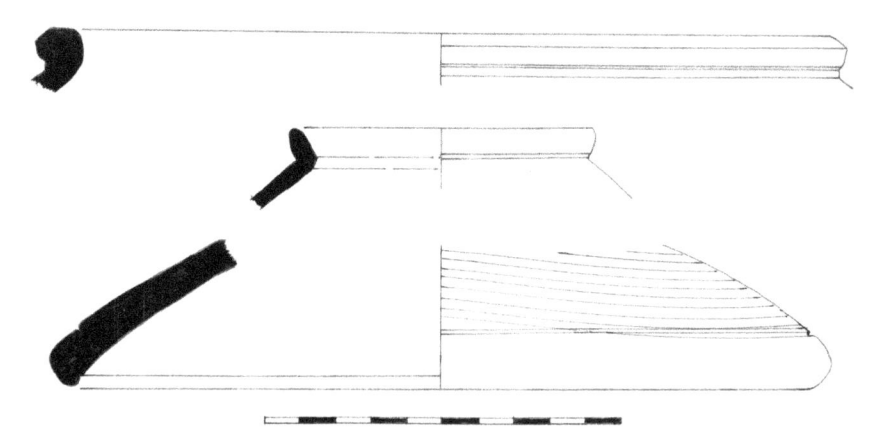

Fig. 23. Drawing of Roman pottery from Holy Well, Little Hinton; rims from a jar, beaker, and lid (scale 10cm)

The name 'Holywell' suggests that it was in use as a medicinal spring in the distant past. In his article 'The Spas and Mineral Springs of Wiltshire' Pafford writes

> The veneration of wells, springs and streams is incredibly old, and this veneration is as natural as their sources of such an important element as water should also be social centres from prehistoric days.[22]

Further pottery fragments were found when archaeological test pits were cut by the authors in the nearby St. Swithun's Churchyard. The sherds from here cover the period from the second century to the fourth century AD and their unworn condition point to habitation in the immediate vicinity.

A similar scenario is evident at Bishopstone where pottery sherds have been found in the churchyard; north of the Church;[23] in quantity northwest of Forty Farm and at Cues Lane where two gullies of Roman date were also revealed during an archaeological evaluation[24]. These find spots lie on either side of the *Lenta* stream watercourse.

At Mount Pleasant Farm, to the north of Little Hinton and straddling the parish boundary, a further farmstead is evidenced by numerous pottery fragments recovered from plough soil. A hoard of silver *denarii* also came from this site.

Roman Pottery

Much of the Roman pottery found in the Parish was made on kiln sites discovered beneath West Swindon and in Savernake Forest[25]. Savernake ware was a widespread industry as kilns producing the wheel-thrown pottery have also been identified on the west side of Martinsell hillfort, near Broomsgrove Farm, at Milton Lilbourne and at Tottenham House near Great Bedwyn. All lie to the south of Marlborough. At Cirencester, their vessels appear in deposits pre-dating AD 55. The challenge of West Swindon wares, amongst others, appear to have caused the gradual demise of the industry in the late second century or at the beginning of the third century AD. Vessels made included: bead rim bowls and jars; necked storage jars and bowls; lids; platters; flagons; campanulate cups and bowls; and flat rimmed dishes.

The West Swindon pottery industry's wheel-thrown products first appear in quantity in deposits dated by imported pottery and coins to AD 100-20, although at the Roman town at Lower Wanborough (*Durocornovium*) it is evidenced as early as AD 60, these may however be products of an earlier kiln site located at Brinkworth.[26] From the mid-third century AD the ware became increasingly important, and manufacture continued into the early years of the fifth century AD.

Fig. 24. Excavating a Roman pottery kiln at Whitehill Farm, West Swindon

Twenty-eight kilns have been evidenced at six locations, other kiln sites are evidenced by wasters and kiln debris. Vessels produced are chiefly: wide mouthed jar; narrow mouthed jar; tankard; lid; flagon; dish and bowl. Also made in smaller numbers were beaker; cooking pot; strainer; mortarium; unguent jar; candlestick; lamp filler; bottle; cheese press; cup; pepper pot and platter.[2]

Other Roman potteries supplying sites in Bishopstone with Little Hinton Parish were kilns in south Dorset, the New Forest, Oxfordshire, the Rhineland, and Central Gaul.

9
Late Roman/Anglo Saxon
(AD 420-850)

Now we are at the beginnings of history as written by the local people of that time. These records were mainly made by monks and peopled by characters with wonderful, unpronounceable names. Be aware they compiled documents mainly to please their masters, but isn't that the case with most of history? Known, for a time, as the Dark Ages (encouraging jokes about too many knights) because of an apparent descent into chaos after the collapse of the Roman Empire, this period is sometimes called sub-Roman. Even the title Anglo/Saxon seems to be falling out of favour, we wish they would stop changing names, it is so confusing. So many questions still not answered. Did King Arthur really exist? What happened to the Romanised Iron Age Brits? We do not know, but archaeology and science are on the case.

The period between the end of Roman rule and the emergence of Saxon kingdoms was a time of conflict and great turmoil. Many regular troops had been withdrawn from Britain to protect Rome's heartland during the latter years of the fourth century AD and in the early years of the fifth century AD. Various usurpers had also been declared Emperor in Britain by the military, so this meant that troops accompanied the usurpers to the continent whilst they sought advancement in territory and power in Gaul and beyond. Amongst these usurpers were Magnus Maximus (AD 383-8), Marcus (AD 406-7), Gratian (AD 407) and Constantine III (AD 407-11). Few if any of these troops returned. Consequently, the country's defences were much weakened at a time when the regular and militia armed forces were trying to repel raids by Germanic warriors on the south-east coast, Pictish warriors to the north and to the west Celtic warriors from Ireland. Objects of Germanic origin, notably military belt fittings found within cemeteries, suggest that leaders of towns in eastern Britain began to hire foreign mercenaries to aid their defence. Most of these people would have brought their families with them and were provided with land to settle on.

Map 8

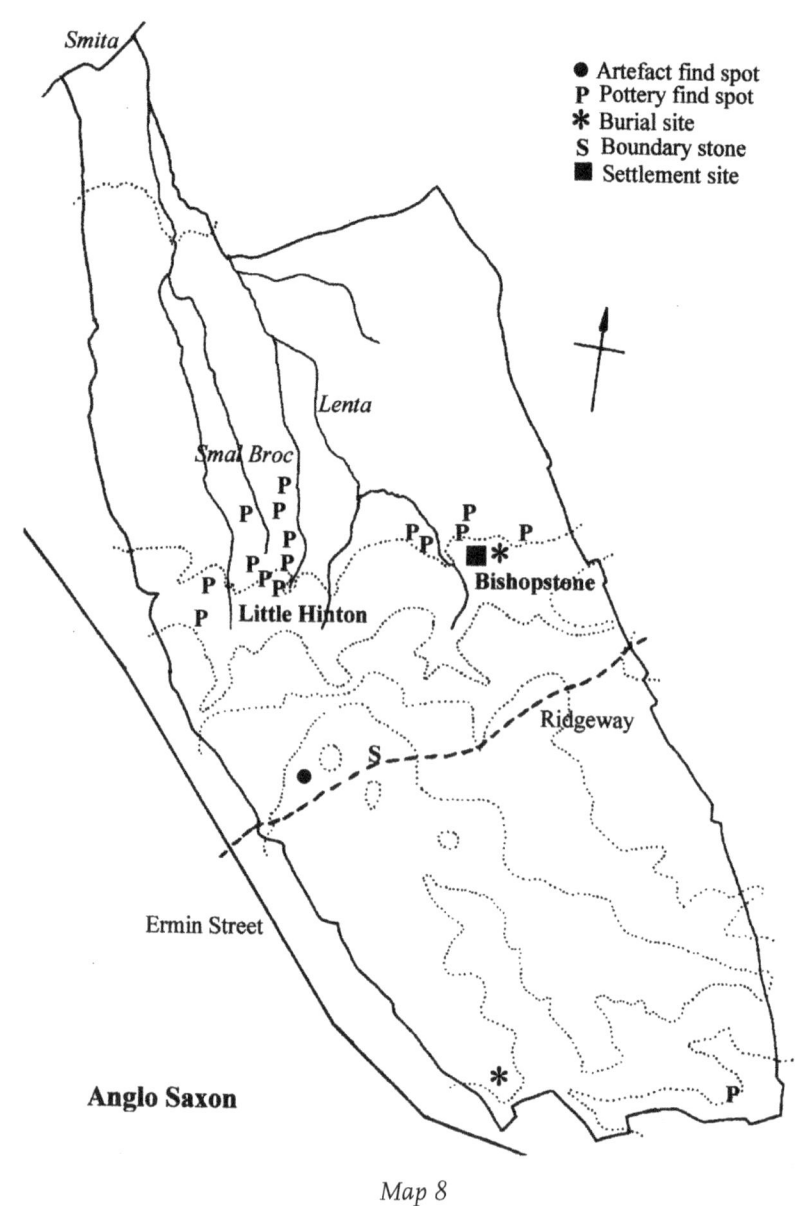

Settlement is evidenced by finds, by us and others, at Little Hinton and Bishopstone, their location clearly being forerunners for the present-day spring-line villages. Elsewhere finds are few and are confined to the southern chalk land – a single sherd from a former Roman villa site, a warrior burial in a Bronze Age barrow and a disc brooch, perhaps an indicator for a cemetery site in a field known as Bone Hill.

Like other towns and many villas in the *Britannia Prima* province, late coinage at the nearby town of *Durocornovium* is present in large numbers in direct contrast to elsewhere in the country. This may well signify the presence in this provincial border town of a military force, since coinage normally entered general circulation from soldiers' pay. Another indication of such a force are distinctive brooches and belt fittings found within the province. Many of the latter depict stylised animals; some decorated with horse heads may imply the existence of mounted militia.

The End of Roman Britain
Britain had stopped minting its own coinage in AD 326 and so relied thereafter on Gaulish mints for supply. The issue of bronze coins to Britain ceased in AD 402 and silver and gold coins in AD 406. Consequently, coinage in circulation dwindled and this resulted in the breakdown of a functioning monetary system that had been relied on to pay for goods, services, and taxes. People now had to rely on self-subsistence, barter, or bullion to survive. Therefore, mass production industries such as pottery manufacture ceased to operate. Skilled workers such as masons, carpenters, mosaicists, and metal workers could not be paid, which resulted in the structural decay and eventual collapse of buildings, particularly those built of stone. Undoubtedly a breakdown in Government control and social order quickly followed. Further deterioration within the settlements and on the villas occurred due to the raiding war-bands, brigand activity and periods of plague. Added to this unstable situation, foreign mercenaries hired by the leaders of towns in eastern Britain rebelled against their employers. Thus, further destabilised, Britain's defences were unable to repel Germanic tribes – Saxons, Jutes and Angles – who seeking fertile land on which to settle joined with the rebels. The numbers of these incomers are debatable, but they were sufficiently large enough to introduce a new language the basis of which we speak today.[28] Clearly land was taken, and the former owners were either slaughtered, enslaved, or driven out while lesser folk such as the tenants of the former landowners may have submitted to the newcomers' rule, simply swapping one property-owner for another. Gildas, a British cleric, penned a sermon '*De Excidio et Conquestu Britanniae*'. Although written over a hundred years after the events, the

Fig. 25. Liddington Castle Iron Age hillfort, refortified in the fifth century AD

sermon records some grains of truth regarding the happenings of that traumatic period. He notes

> All the major towns were laid low by the repeated battering of enemy rams and laid low too all the inhabitants – church leaders, priests, and people alike as the swords glinted all around and the flames crackled.

Self-subsistence for the remaining Romano-British people was easier to achieve in the countryside where arable land was available, so partial, or total abandonment of large settlements took place. Notably some hillforts such as Liddington Castle appear to have been refortified at this time suggesting that some of the local population had retired to them as places of safety. Gildas records

> ....the cities of our land are not populated even now as they once were; right up to the present they are deserted in ruins and unkempt.

Mount Badon

Many battles followed as the British in the west fought back. Eventually the Saxon advance was halted after defeat by the legendary Arthur and his

Fig. 26. Anglo-Saxon chaff tempered pottery sherds

troops during the three-day siege and battle of *Mons Badonicus* (Mount Badon) in *c*.517 AD. Nennius, a Welsh monk, in his writing *Historia Brittonum c*.800 AD tells us that the mythical Arthur's twelfth battle was on Badon Hill and in it 960 Saxons fell in one day from a single charge by Arthur. A highly likely contender for this battle site is nearby Liddington Castle, which dominates the area between two major Roman roads and overlooks the Ridgeway. Early maps refer to the hill on which the fort stands as Badbury Hill. Nearby is the village of Badbury which is recorded in a Saxon charter of AD 955 as *Baddeburri* (Badda's burh). This name may have originally related to the fortification that dominates the skyline immediately to the southeast of the village.

The fall of Britannia Prima

During this lull in the fighting the Saxons consolidated their realm in the east before again invading mid- and western Britain. The Roman western province of *Britannia Prima*, which archaeological and documentary evidence demonstrates withstood the Saxon advance for a long period of time, finally began to crumble. The *Annales Cambriae* record that Arthur was killed in AD 537 at the Battle of *Camlann* (possibly in Somerset). The British were also defeated in AD 556 at the Battle of *Beranburh* (Barbury Castle) by the forces of Cynric and Ceawlin. Following defeat at the Battle of *Deorham* (Dyrham in South Gloucestershire) in AD 577 the cities of Cirencester, Gloucester and Bath were taken signalling the end of *Britannia Prima*.

The rise of Saxon kingdoms
By the seventh century AD five large Saxon kingdoms had emerged, namely Wessex, Kent, East Anglia, Mercia, and Northumbria. The eighth century AD saw the dominance of the Midlands kingdom of Mercia under King Offa.

Saxon Rule
To achieve effective rule Saxon kingship entailed regular visitation to all parts of the kingdom, which resulted in the establishment of many royal villas (*Villa Regia*). Wessex comprised four shires – Wiltshire; Hampshire; Somerset and Dorset – each named after a settlement that surrounded a royal villa – Wilton, Hampton, Somerton, and Dorchester. Many other royal villas existed within each shire, often attached to a royal estate. Each of these provided the centre for a settlement which took on local administration and served as a market for locally produced

Fig. 27. Anglo-Saxon sunken floored hut excavation in Old Town, Swindon

and imported goods. They also served as a focus for religious events and military organisation.

Saxon Settlement evidence

Evidence for early Saxon occupation in the area is difficult to establish as pottery, the commonest dating material, changed little in form or fabric between the mid-fifth and the late eighth century AD. This handmade pottery, mainly tempered with organic material, was largely undecorated. By the mid-sixth century AD Anglo-Saxon occupation is clearly evidenced, within the region, through datable items of weaponry and jewellery.

Town life was virtually unknown to early Saxons, their settlements largely comprising a cluster of small buildings arranged around a large hall, or as isolated farmsteads. These buildings where traditionally built-in timber, the use of which they were highly skilled in. A common type of building is the sunken floored hut (*grubenhaus*). Several examples of these were found at Harlstone House in Bishopstone during an excavation in advance of building work[29]. These wattle and daub walled structures, constructed within rectangular hollows dug into the ground, are considered to be storage and work-related buildings. A burial of the same period was also found. The present curving road layout around the site strongly suggest that it lay within a defended royal enclosure. Around the village further Saxon sherds have been recovered through excavation, construction, and archaeological fieldwork. A similar settlement seems to exist at Little Hinton as archaeological test pits, cut in St. Swithun's Churchyard, produced chaff tempered pottery sherds. A little northwest of the church two further pottery sherds were found in spoil derived from the cutting of a post pit and a small trench cut north of the manor produced another sherd. Many other Saxon pottery

Fig. 28. Anglo-Saxon saucer brooch from Bone Hill field (diam. 4cm)

fragments have been found scattered around the village indicative of night soil and farmyard waste spread that had been used to fertilise the fields. Away from the two villages only a few Saxon pottery sherds have been found; one came from the Roman villa site at Russley Park, hinting at continued activity on the site, the others from Hinton Downs. On this down an Anglo-Saxon warrior had been interred, equipped with an iron headed spear, in a grave cut into a Bronze Age bowl barrow. Southwest of Charlbury Hill a possible Saxon cemetery site is hinted at by the finding of a gilt bronze saucer brooch having traces of fabric on the underside and the field name – 'Bone Hill'.

10
Early Medieval
(AD 850-1066)

Now, where have we got to? Let us reflect. 10,000 years ago, this land was roamed by groups of hunter-gathers. About 4,000 years later saw the introduction of new ideas of farming, permanency, and land ownership. And after a further 2,500 years they were smelting metal and, by 700BC, smithing iron. Were these all the same people? Who knows? Next the Roman legionaries arrived to change things completely. However, they only lasted about 400 years and withdrew leaving the chaos of the last chapter. Now we have the kingdoms and battles as recorded in the Anglo-Saxon Chronicle.

Warning action alert – those nasty barbarians in long ships from across the North Sea have arrived on the scene and are bringing terror to all and sundry. Bury your treasures and lock up your daughters, but do not worry King Alfred is coming to the rescue.

Now read on...

Mid ninth-century AD England comprised four independent Kingdoms – Mercia, Northumbria, East Anglia, and Wessex. Norse incursions into northern and western Britain commenced at the end of the eighth century AD. These led to Norse settlement in AD 865 following invasion of Northumbria and capture of York by a great Norse army led jointly by Guthrum, Ivar the Boneless, his brother Halfdan and Ubbe Ragnarsson. A few years later two Norse armies, one led by Bagsecg and the other by Halfdan, invaded central and southern England. A planned assault on Wessex in AD 871 was defeated at the battle of Ashdown by the forces of King Alfred who ruled from AD 871 to AD 899. This battle site is thought to lie on the Ridgeway near Wantage in Oxfordshire. Bagsecg was killed and the routed army retired to northern England. Attacks continued though and by AD 876 only Wessex remained whole. But the Danish leader Guthrum continued to attack Wessex and eventually, on Epiphany 6 January AD 878 he launched a surprise night-time attack on Alfred and his court at the fortified town

Fig. 29. King Alfred the Great

of Chippenham, Wiltshire. Utterly defeated, Alfred and his surviving troops fled from the battle to take refuge in the Somerset marshes. There he built-up and armed a new army. Alfred subsequently defeated a great army led by Guthrum in May AD 878 at the Battle of *Ethandun*, thought to be at Edington in North Wiltshire. Guthrum and the remains of his army retreated to Chippenham. Here he was besieged by Alfred and after two weeks Guthrum, on the verge of starvation, sued for peace.

Saxon Towns

Part of Alfred's successful defence of Wessex had been achieved through the placing throughout Wessex of fortified towns (*Burhs*) defended by 27,000 warriors. This enabled the rural populace to retire to them for safety during Norse raids. Bishopstone with Little Hinton Parish is in what was the northernmost part of Wessex, the River Thames being the border between Wessex and Mercia. The nearest fortified town was that of Cricklade set on the southern bank of the River Thames. Others nearby include the Wiltshire town of Malmesbury and Wallingford in Oxfordshire. The towns brought about major changes. Scattered farming communities saw in their midst the creation of an urban-based society not known since the end of Roman rule over four hundred years earlier. Inhabitants of burhs constituted an increasingly important class, who exercised rights of justice and land-lordship. These townsfolk, having strong royal military and ecclesiastical interests, represented an elitist element which supplied the market with a widening range of goods and helped create the demand for items produced both locally and further afield. Now people who had gained varied skills rather than continuing to make a living from agricultural activity, found they could set up in specific trades like metal, wood, leather, bone and horn working, textile manufacture, as shop and inn keepers, potters or even as moneyers.

Increasing Wessex Power
Offensives by Wessex, aided by Mercian forces, and increasing raids from Denmark, ultimately weakened Norse military power in the north. This led to their submission to Edward the Elder (born c. AD 874-7, died AD 924) in return for protection, resulting in the north becoming part of Edward's England.

Danish Supremacy
King Aethelred (born c. AD 968, died 1016) feared a resurgence of Norse and Danish power in England, and in the year 1000 he plundered the Isle of Man and parts of the Anglo-Scandinavian north to try to crush the independently minded Scandinavians living there. His continuing fear finally led, in 1002, to him ordering the massacre of all Danish men living in England. In revenge Svein Forkbeard from Denmark brought an army to England and raided south and east England throughout 1003/4, but a famine in England forced Svein to take his army back to Denmark in 1005. He continued raiding until 1013 when he returned, with his son Canute, intending to conquer England. This he achieved and Aethelred fled to Normandy. The following year Svein died and Aethelred came back and expelled the Danes, now under Canute's leadership. In August 1015 Canute returned and in the following year, at the Battle of *Assandun* (Ashingdon or Ashdon in Essex), defeated Edmund II (born AD 989, died 1016), Aethelred's third son and successor. A treaty was drawn up in which Canute took control of northern England and Edmund the south. Canute soon found himself the first Danish king of all England as Edmund died shortly after signing the treaty. Canute proved to be a good king, ruling justly, building churches and, as he also ruled the Danish homelands, he was able to protect England against attacks. He died in 1035 and was buried at Winchester.

Early Medieval Evidence

The spurious charter of AD 854 regarding Hinton Parish (see introduction) refers to various features such as sarsen boundary stones, coombs and the rivers which can still be seen in the landscape, although others such as a crooked apple tree have obviously long since vanished. The River *Lenta* is the stream that was part of the eastern boundary and *Smita* is the Cole. Some of the boundary stones have individual names such as *Har Stan* (grey, hoary or old stone) or *Hol Stan* (a stone with a hole in it).

Part of this estate included Earlscourt, excavations here in advance of building construction revealed ditches associated with Saxo-Norman pottery (AD 950-1150). Such pottery has been found in the fortress towns of Malmesbury and Cricklade, notably tall narrow handmade cooking pots in a coarse limestone fabric, produced in potters' workshops in or near the two towns early in their existence. Similar pottery fragments of ninth to tenth century AD date were found north of Hinton Copse during field walking.

Fig. 30. Sarsen boundary marker, the Har Stan, on Hinton Downs

II
Medieval
(AD 1066-1485)

1066 and 1485, two important dates in English history (if we are still allowed to say English?). It is said that every schoolboy, sorry school person, knows the former date, but hands up who remembers what happened in 1485? If you do not know you will have to read chapter 12.

Spoiler alert. If the thought of class systems makes you weep, do not read the social order bit.

Norman Conquest
William Duke of Normandy (born c.1028, died 1087) in 1066 laid claim to the English crown following the death of Edward the Confessor. However, Harold Godwinson (born c.1022 died 1066) had been crowned first. William gathered an army and set sail, landing on the south coast. When he heard of William's invasion Harold had just defeated his brother Tostig, another claimant to the throne, and his supporter the Norwegian King Haradrada and his army at Stamford Bridge. Harold and his men hurried to confront the threat and in the ensuing Battle at Hastings Harold was killed and the English army was beaten. William was crowned on Christmas Day 1066 at Westminster Abbey despite continued resistance, mostly in the north. This led, in the winter of 1069-70 to the 'Harrying of the North' when William's army burnt whole villages, slaughtered the inhabitants, destroyed livestock and food stores, and salted the land. Of the people who escaped the carnage it is said that 100,000 later died of hunger and some even resorted to cannibalism.

Medieval Social Order
William, as king, headed a social pyramid with un-free peasants at the bottom. Noblemen received from the king gifts of land in return for military support (*knight's fee*). The aristocracy in turn had ordinary freemen bonded to them by similar ties. This was the system known as feudalism, essential to which was the concept of the manor, which

Map 9

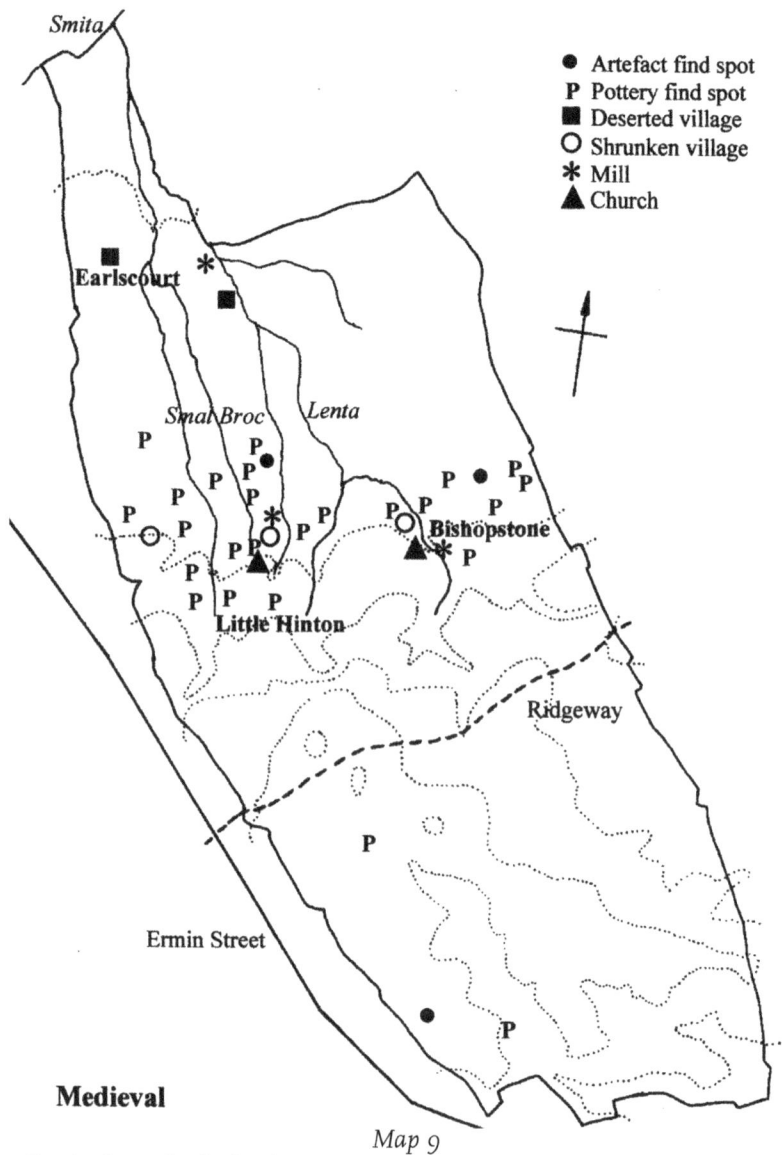

Clearly from the finds' distribution, as the map shows, the two spring-line villages had become well established complete with churches and mills in the medieval period. Surrounding the villages, defined by spreads of worn pottery fragments derived from amongst night soil and farmyard waste used as fertilizer for crops, and surviving as ridge and furrow and lynchets in the combes, were the settlements fields. The lack of finds by us on the southern chalk land suggest that they were largely used for the grazing of sheep for much of the period. To the north, on the clay land, two small villages are evidenced by pottery sherds and crop marks, one associated with a manor and the other with a mill.

released knights from work on their farms to fight for the king. Work was carried out on the manor, usually containing a single village, by the tenants who held lands from the lord and who were given protection in return for service on his or her land. *Villeins* (villagers) made up the main element of a settlement's population. They swore fealty to their lord but enjoyed no rights under common law. The lord could evict them from their fields, increase rents or impose *tallage* (tax) on them as he saw fit. Despite this, they could become successful farmers, holding between ten and forty acres. Below *villeins* were *cottars* (cottagers), who had no more than five acres and whose dues to the lord were different. A *cottar* might work as a ploughman for his lord in return for the right to use his lord's plough and team. *Bordars* (smallholders), middle class peasants, usually had more land than a *cottar* but less than a *villein*. Superior to *villeins* were freemen, but legal free status did not necessarily mean superior wealth, as a rich *villein* could employ a poor freeman. Their dues to the lord tended to be of a more administrative order. The lowest was a slave who owed personal service to another and could not move home, work, change allegiance, or buy or sell without permission.

A picture of the existing settlements is presented by the Domesday Book of 1086, a pattern that is still identifiable today. Commissioned by King William this survey of all the land and resources in his realm, was to know what financial and military resources could be drawn on. Varying greatly in size, late eleventh-century English manorial estates followed an ancient pattern of isolated farms, hamlets and tiny villages scattered over most of the cultivatable land. The old patchwork pattern of small rectangular fields established in the Bronze Age gave way to an open field system. In this system large unenclosed fields were divided into furlongs of around 200m wide and 220m long, which were further subdivided into long narrow strips called selions or ridges that consisted of about 0.2 hectares (0.5 acres). These strips are commonly known as ridge and furrow, and examples of these can still be seen in pasture around Hinton Copse, north of Little Hinton.

Local Churches
Within Bishopstone Parish two medieval villages have survived into modern times, Bishopstone and Little Hinton. Located in them are the churches of St. Mary's and St. Swithun's.

Fig. 31. St. Mary's Church, Bishopstone

In Bishopstone St Mary's, built in the perpendicular style, is mainly fifteenth century in date with traces of thirteenth/fourteenth century construction. It was heavily restored in 1868 and 1883. The building, built of random rubble and ashlar blocks on a moulded plinth, has at the west end a tower which is crennelated, and has diagonal buttresses and three set offs above plinth level. Its belfry, with its two light and trefoil windows, is reached via an angled stair turret on the south-east corner. Its west door built 1883 has Tudor arch trimmings and a large three light perpendicular style window above. A three-bay aisled nave has stepped buttresses, whilst a lower two bay chancel has stepped diagonal buttresses. It is lit by two and three light square headed windows with labels and foiled heads and a two-light clerestory on the south side. To the north the aisle windows have set back chamfer surrounds and, adjacent, the porch entrance appears to date circa 1200. In the chancel wall is a very ornate reset small Norman doorway with horizontal chevron ornament. The east window of the south aisle has early C14 reticulated tracery. Above the aisles are quatrefoil parapets. Internally the nave has a three-bay, four-centred arcade (one bay shorter

left: Fig. 32. Twelfth century carved stone corbel on the church's south interior wall

above: Fig. 33. Sundial on the south exterior wall of Bishopstone Church

to north due to the porch) with undulating section to the column shafts. Set into the south wall are three carved stone masks that are perhaps twelfth century in date? Of late Norman date the font has a tongued scalloped bowl set on a dog-tooth fillet with six columns forming the stem. Fragments of mediaeval stained glass also survive. Examination of disturbed soil in the churchyard resulted in the finding of eighteen medieval pottery sherds and a roof ridge tile fragment.

In the northwest corner of Little Hinton village, fronted by a miniature green, stands the village church that was first recorded in 1172 when the Bishop of Winchester confirmed St. Swithun's Priory as its patron. It is built of rubble with ashlar dressings and comprises a chancel, an aisled and clerestoried nave with south porch, and a west tower. The nave is earlier than its arcades and along with the tower dates to the late Saxon/early Norman period. The arcades of two bays have long spans; that to the south is of the later twelfth century in date whilst the northern dates to the early twelfth century. East-facing windows were inserted in both aisles in the thirteenth century and are probably of their original dimensions. The chancel arch was reconstructed in the earlier thirteenth century. The chancel itself, however, was rebuilt a century later and retains three contemporary windows and a priest's doorway. Of late Saxon or early Norman date the base of the west tower is

Fig. 34. St Swithun's Church, Little Hinton

contemporary with the west nave wall. Its upper stages, surmounted by a tiled pyramidal roof, may have been rebuilt in the fourteenth century. The clerestory was added in the early sixteenth century when the nave was re-roofed and is lit by square-headed windows of three lights. At the same time windows as those in the clerestory were inserted in the aisle walls, and a south porch was constructed. A collection of late thirteenth century encaustic floor tiles was recorded recently in the south aisle. They are attributable to the Wessex School tilery whose kilns, based on distribution lie in the Salisbury area. Although much worn, the tiles can be seen to depict hybrids (man-headed birds), floral motifs, interlocking circles, shields, triangles and the 'Green Man'. It is considered that in medieval art the 'Green Man' depicted partly concealed by foliage is meant as a warning about the devil's entrapment of the unwary[30]. Of particular interest is that within Bishopstone Church there are exact Victorian copies, made by Minton, of the 'Green Man' tile. Apparently two identical medieval tiles depicting the 'Green Man' had also been found at Bishopstone during restoration work.[31] The font in the church dates to the early Norman period and is one of the most remarkable in

Fig. 35, Drawings of and actual Medieval tiles in St. Swithun's Church, apart from the 19th century tile (bottom right) from St. Mary's Bishopstone

Fig. 36. Details from the font showing a bird and a wolf with a vine issuing from its mouth and an entwined serpent, fish, and birds

Fig. 37. Test pit revealing the stone foundations of St Swithun's Church tower

the county. It is ornately carved depicting a band of arched columns above a zone of entwined cord within which a panel portrays a vine issuing from a wolf's mouth supported by a hand from above, a goose, three birds, a coiled serpent and two fish.

Three test pits cut external to the late Saxon/early Norman tower wall revealed it had a sandstone chamfered plinth which overlay massive sarsen foundations one metre plus in depth. Finds included many medieval pottery sherds.

A manor house at Bishopstone stood to the west of the church and to the rear of Prebendal Farm. It was recorded in 1647 as being a ten-room house, built of and roofed with stone, with thatched outbuildings. There is no evidence for a medieval manor house at Hinton though. Manor Farm, regarded as the manor, is set into a slight depression immediately north of the church and dates from the seventeenth century. It may conceal the remains of 'the farm of the monastic community' and which was overseen by the larger estate held by the Winchester monastic community at Wanborough.

Mills

In medieval times another important structure would have been a mill for the grinding of grain into flour. No trace of such a structure has yet been located with certainty for the medieval period, although post-medieval mills are evidenced in both villages (see next chapter). A document (Pleas of juries and assizes at Wilton) refers in 1249 to a Bishopstone miller called Ralph. Ralph fled to the church seeking sanctuary when Walter Algar, who suffered from falling sickness (epilepsy?), suddenly fell dead. The jurors at the Assizes found him not guilty of the death, so he was acquitted. Other documents record four mills in the village during the mid-fourteenth century and two in the early fifteenth century.[32]

Fig. 38. Medieval overshot mill depicted in the fourteenth century Luttrell Psalter

Not identifiable to a named post-medieval mill or location on Hinton's manorial *demesne* a mill is mentioned in 1248. It was repaired in 1273 and its house in 1280. In both years, the miller received 5s. In 1281 the mill was leased for 10 years at £1 4s yearly[33]. A mill called Berry Mill is mentioned in 1419 as being attached to the manorial estate.

Settlements

Peasants lived in small timber-framed cottages usually with a garden for growing vegetables such as cabbage, peas and leeks or herbs, or on larger plots in longhouses that were constructed in either stone, timber, wattle and daub, clay, or a combination of them. In a longhouse oxen occupied one end and humans the other, separated by a cross passage. Outside there may have been a barn, workshop, garden, animal pens and orchard. In the Wiltshire Crown Pleas of 1249, it is recorded that evildoers' unknown came by night to the house of Ralph of Hinton and robbed him.[34]

Some villages have completely disappeared from the landscape, only being identifiable as mounds and hollows in pasture or cropmarks in ploughed fields and, sometimes, associated with a surviving farmhouse or two. These have been given the title 'deserted medieval villages', or if more than three inhabited buildings exist amongst the remains 'shrunken medieval villages'. Research has shown that abandonment of villages occurred mainly in the fifteenth century. At this time fields that had been cultivated for cereals and vegetables by villagers were being turned into sheep pasture by the landowners to supply the very profitable wool trade. Consequently only a few shepherds were needed to care for the animals. Other contributory factors that led to abandonment were soil exhaustion and disease, notably plague.

The 'Black Death' was one of the most devastating pandemics in human history. It is widely considered to have been an outbreak of bubonic plague and to have originated in China. Carried along the Silk Road by infected travellers it reached the Crimea by 1346 and then, carried by fleas residing on black rats it spread

Fig. 39. Thirteenth century manuscript depiction of a rat and a cat

throughout the Mediterranean region and Europe. During the summer months of 1348 the first outbreak swept across the south of England in bubonic form, before mutating into the even more terrifying pneumonic form with the commencement of winter. It is estimated to have killed around 10-15% of the population. By the end of 1350 it had subsided, but never fully died out. Outbreaks continued throughout the remainder of the fourteenth century and much of the fifteenth century. In 1471 it again killed around 10-15% of the population, while the plague death rate of 1479 and 1480 may have been as high as 20%.

Medieval Settlements in the Parish
A 'deserted medieval village' is evidenced to the south of Hinton Marsh Farm, near a later mill site. It was initially evidenced through aerial photographs as linear earthworks in a grassed field, but unfortunately it has since been ploughed. Walking over the site evidenced many twelfth to fifteenth century pottery sherds, a whetstone, animal bones and much building stone.

Another deserted medieval village is indicated north of Earlscourt Farm by numerous pottery sherds found in plough soil over an extensive area and in archaeological evaluation trenches cut prior to tree planting. Aerial photographs here show linear features in growing crops. Earlscourt Farm itself was recorded, in a document dated to 1423 as comprising a hall, two chambers, a barn, a stable and a sheepfold.

Both Bishopstone and Little Hinton can be designated as 'shrunken medieval villages' as recently earthworks have been noted to the north of the present settlements. Observation by the authors at Little Hinton of a trench being cut through the earthworks that comprise platforms, hollows and a hollow way revealed stone footings of two medieval buildings.[35] Also found were numerous animal bones, thirteenth- to fourteenth-century pottery fragments and whetstones. The presence here of sheep and cattle bones fits in well with the historical documentary evidence, for example in 1210 when over 200 sheep of various types and ten cows, as well as numerous calves were accounted for on the *demesne*. In 1248 the *demesne* ewe and lamb flocks were large and included 115 lambs sent from Winchester Priory's estate at Wroughton. Fleeces from 537 sheep and 144 lambs were recorded at Hinton in 1273. The heavy clay soils in the northern third of the Hinton

Parish supported herds of cows. Ten cows, as well as numerous calves, were accounted for on the *demesne* in 1210[36]. The presence, as indicated by the bones of mainly mature animals, show that they were not raised solely for meat, but mostly for long term products – wool from sheep and milk from cows. Demonstrated for the latter is the recording that in 1273 on the *demesne* 38 winter and 173 summer cheeses were produced.[37] The number of bones gnawed by dogs is high, telling that the animal was common on the site, presumably used as watch dogs, for hunting game and rounding up of stock.

Similar evidence to that found at little Hinton was obtained in a trial excavation by the authors at Bishopstone. Here, overlooking the *Lenta* stream and lying amongst earthworks a late thirteenth- to late fourteenth-century semi-sunken stone-walled building was partly excavated. In its south-west corner an infant's burial was encountered. Infants buried in this way in medieval times were consistent with the status of a non-person. Non-persons included murderers, suicides and the unbaptised and as such could not be buried in a churchyard. Adjacent to the building, evidence for iron smelting and smithing was discovered in the form of slag, a hearth and furnace debris. A smithy, where agricultural equipment could be manufactured and repaired, horses shod, and weapons, nails, household items and building fittings forged, would have existed in most medieval villages. Following the demise of the building and ceasing of the blacksmith's activity occupation clearly continued, shown by the build-up of compacted loam and chalk fragment layer that underlay the topsoil. From it came late fourteenth- to sixteenth-century fine glazed vessel fragments and

Fig. 40. Excavation of a late 13th- to late 14th-century building at Bishopstone with an infant burial in the corner

Fig. 41. Medieval manuscript depicting a blacksmith's smithy

animal bone. Of the latter the whole range of body parts are apparent, although there appears to be a lack of cranial, spinal, and pelvic portions suggesting that much of the meat arrived, at least on this part of the site, as leg joints. The presence here of many sheep and cattle bones, like that at Little Hinton, complements the documentary evidence. In 1341 the *demesne* land included a *carucate* of arable, meadowland and several pastures for 100 sheep and 14 cattle. In 1425 at Michaelmas there were flocks of 379 wethers (castrated male sheep) and 311 ewes. Some 652 sheep were kept in 1428[38]. This increase in sheep rearing, common throughout the county, would have reduced the number of tenants required on the manor as cultivated land made way for pasture, and consequently a reduction in the number of dwellings.

Within the present village, at Cue's Lane, recent excavation, prior to development, has revealed three eleventh- to thirteenth-century ditched enclosures and a well that was infilled prior to the fourteenth century. Excavation at Harlstone House also revealed medieval features.

Another area of shrunken settlement is recorded around West Hinton Farm, *Westhyneton* in AD 1334. Possible house platforms are visible here on an aerial photograph as slight earthworks.

Around the villages, chiefly Little Hinton, field walking following ploughing has revealed extensive scatters of medieval pottery sherds.

These undoubtedly are the result of the spreading of night soil and farmyard waste as fertiliser. Old aerial photographs and some still extant examples demonstrate the extent and layout of these former fields. Shortage of land encouraged farmers to create fields on the steep slopes of the coombes that lie to the south of Bishopstone and Little Hinton. Known as strip-lynchets they form a series of steep terraced surfaces and are popularly called 'Shepherd's Steps'. Another way of fertilising the fields was to provide fresh dung to enrich the thin chalk land soils for growing wheat and barley. At night, the shepherd would pen the vast flocks of sheep in a fold made from hurdles, and each day he would move them on so that eventually the whole field was covered.

Fig. 42. Ridge and furrow' strip fields in pasture in nearby Liddington Parish

Enclosures

Within Bishopstone Parish and the surrounding north-east Wiltshire parishes, many large circular or sub-circular banked enclosures with an internal ditch have been identified, chiefly through aerial photography. Some are in groups. Most lie in the adjacent former Highworth

Hundred, consequently it is highly likely that they originated there, either from local custom or agricultural practise. Few have been investigated, one that has was sited at Stratton Park, adjacent to Ermin Street. In 1975/6, prior to destruction by road construction, excavation showed it to have a very narrow south facing entrance and was of late medieval date[39]. Animal bones recovered comprised chiefly sheep, but also include horse, dog, and cattle. It has been suggested that they were used for the impounding of animals that have strayed or been found grazing illegally. However, their size, and the total recorded (around sixty) seem too much for that sole purpose. It is clear though that these earthworks, with an inner ditch and presumably the outer bank topped with hurdles or a hedge, were constructed as pens for temporarily holding animals. They would have been chiefly useful at sheep shearing time, lambing, penning animals at night-time, or gathering animals prior to driving them to market. Within Bishopstone Parish a cluster of these enclosures appear to have existed to the south and south-east of Hinton Marsh Farm. Another has been noted recently west of Starveall Farm.

Fig. 43. Medieval silver coins from Bishopstone

Pottery

Based on the medieval pottery found, kilns in the Kennet Valley appear to have been supplying the area with coarse ware vessels from the eleventh century, or perhaps earlier, and continued to do so until the early fifteenth century. In competition potters at Minety in North Wiltshire and on Selsley Common in Gloucestershire provided vessels to the village from the thirteenth century into the fifteenth century and then, following the demise of the Kennet Valley industry, into the sixteenth century. Kennet Valley Ware is found across a wide area of west Berkshire and north-east Wiltshire. First identified and defined in archaeological deposits in Newbury[40] it was named as 'Kennet Valley ware' following the discovery of a kiln site near the town[41]. The basic vessel forms (jars, dishes, and bowls) show only a limited degree of morphological development over the production period. Minety[42] and Selsley Common[43] wares included pans, jugs, cisterns, pipkins, lids, shallow dishes, bowls, and bottles, as well as roof ridge tiles. Occasionally their vessels and tiles were decorated with wavy combing in horizontal bands, and many bore a thin patchy olive lead glaze coating.

A small number of fine ware vessels, mainly decorated glazed jugs, were supplied from distant kiln sites in the later medieval period and into the sixteenth century. Seemingly the chief supplier of these was

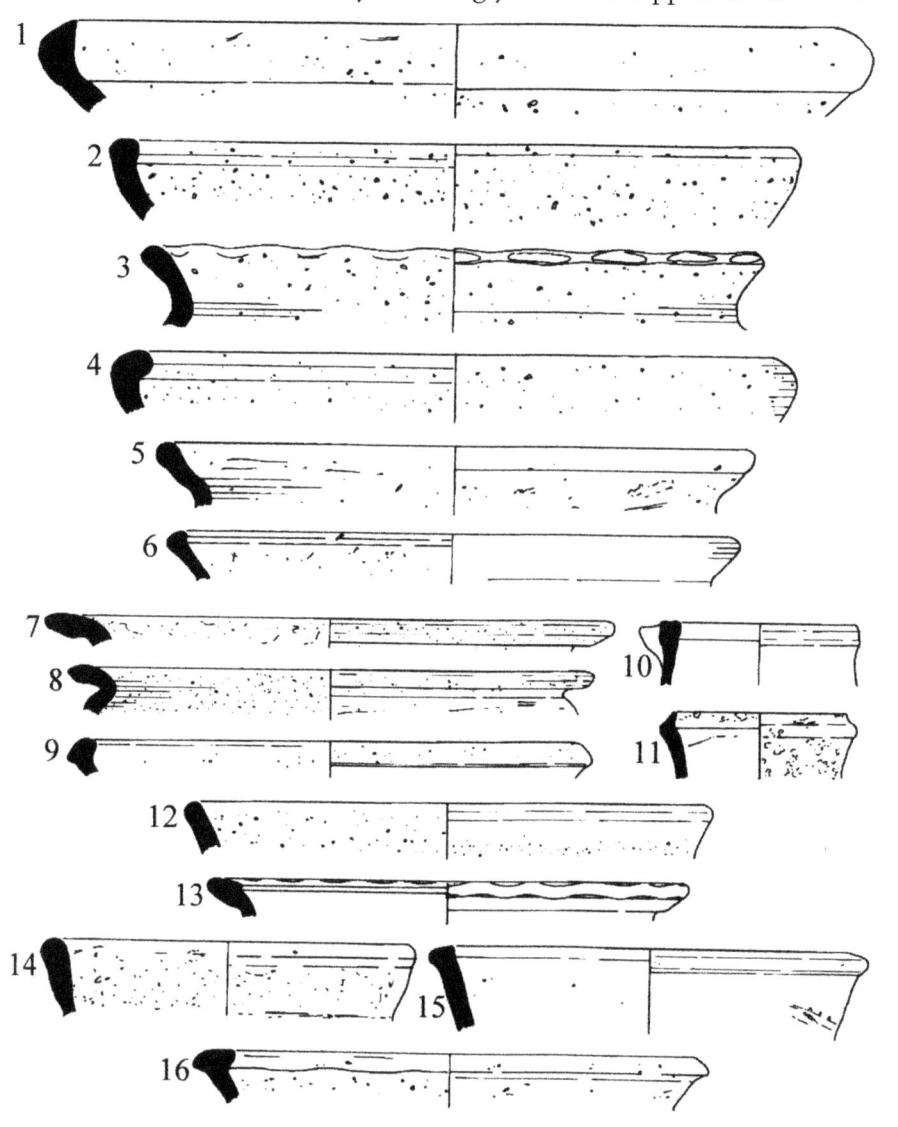

Fig. 44. Rim profiles of medieval pottery found north of Bishopstone Church

1; Kennet Valley ware dish rim, mid twelfth to fourteenth century
2; Kennet Valley ware dish rim, mid twelfth to fourteenth century
3; Kennet Valley ware cooking pot rim, thumb impressed on top, mid twelfth to fourteenth century
4; Kennet Valley ware dish rim, mid twelfth to fourteenth century
6; Coarse Border ware pipkin or cauldron rim, late fourteenth to early sixteenth century
7; Minety/Selsey Common ware cooking pot rim, thirteenth to early sixteenth century
8; Minety/Selsey Common ware cooking pot rim, thirteenth to early sixteenth century
9; Coarse Border ware pipkin or cauldron rim, late fourteenth to early sixteenth century
10; Jug rim, fourteenth to early sixteenth century
11; Coarse Border ware jug rim, late fourteenth to early sixteenth century
12; Kennet Valley ware cooking pot rim, mid twelfth to fourteenth century
13; Kennet Valley ware cooking pot rim, thumb impressed edge, mid twelfth to fourteenth century
14; Kennet Valley ware cooking pot rim, mid twelfth to fourteenth century
15; Coarse Border ware pipkin or cauldron rim, late fourteenth to early sixteenth century
16; Kennet Valley ware cooking pot rim, mid twelfth to fourteenth century

the 'Coarse Border' potteries.[44] This industry is located on the Surrey-Hampshire border. Its products are chiefly found over much of north-east Hampshire and west Surrey. Dating for the commencement of this ware, on present evidence, is the early thirteenth century. By the mid-fourteenth century its products had begun to appear in London and south-east England in large quantities, and examples are now being recognised in much of north-east Wiltshire. Courseware production seemingly ceased in the early sixteenth century, but its fine wares, developed in the late fourteenth century continued to be made, notably thin-walled green glazed cups and jugs. Some vessels, particularly pipkins and cauldrons, only had a light glaze on the base internally.

Fig. 45. Fragments of medieval pottery from a kiln site at Minety in North Wiltshire

12
Post-Medieval
(1485 – 1900)

Here we are at the start of an era that would eventually lead to an industrialised World. Not for the better some would say. Life at this time had continued in our two villages and its surrounding countryside with little change for hundreds of years and it was going to be the same for hundreds of years more with a few incidents to enliven the drudgery of daily existence.

The medieval period is considered to have ended with the defeat, by Henry VII, of Richard III at the Battle of Bosworth Field in 1485. Henry made England a prosperous country and when he died in 1509 his son's (Henry VIII) succession was not challenged, so the Tudor dynasty was established. Throughout this period and into the Industrial Revolution little change was to be seen within the Parish.

Village and Farm
Around 1647-9 there were about 50 farmsteads with small areas of pasture in Bishopstone and 1,750 acres of arable land in the centre of the parish. North of that, all the lowland meadows and pasture seem to have been used in common, and the upland used as common pasture for cattle. Of the *demesne* farm of Bishopstone Manor 750-800 acres were in the western half of the parish, seventy yardlands (1,450 acres) were held by forty-two copyholders, with each yardland having feeding rights for thirty sheep, two horses and three beasts. Common husbandry in Bishopstone was in general altered little in the 18th century although it was constantly being refined and amended in detail. Before 1758, however, 120 acres of Russley Down was inclosed and made into a sporting estate. There were then forty-one farmsteads in the village and only a down land barn outside it. In 1784, when the parish measured 3,520 acres there were 1,725 acres of arable land, over 700 acres of meadow and lowland pasture, and over 800 acres of upland pasture and down. Of the arable land 441 acres were sown with wheat, 254 acres

ITS ARCHAEOLOGY AND HISTORY 69

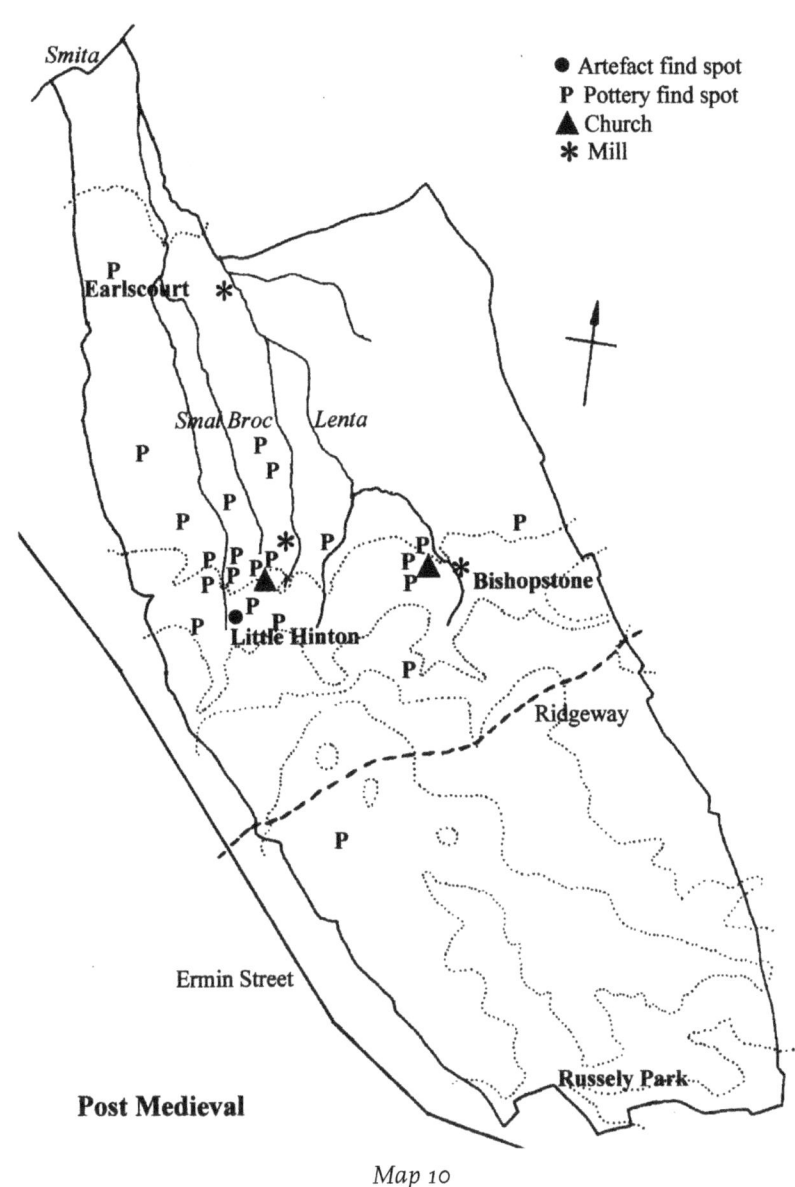

Map 10
Little change is demonstrated in the distribution of our finds from the medieval era for this period. The two spring line villages largely comprise of a cluster of farms with a few shops, blacksmiths, mills, inns, and churches. The two small villages on the northern clay land have vanished although the manor buildings remain and the mill, formerly built adjacent to a farm, is rebuilt a short distance away. Activity on the southern down land, as demonstrated by finds, is still slight apart from the establishing of a lodge at Russley.

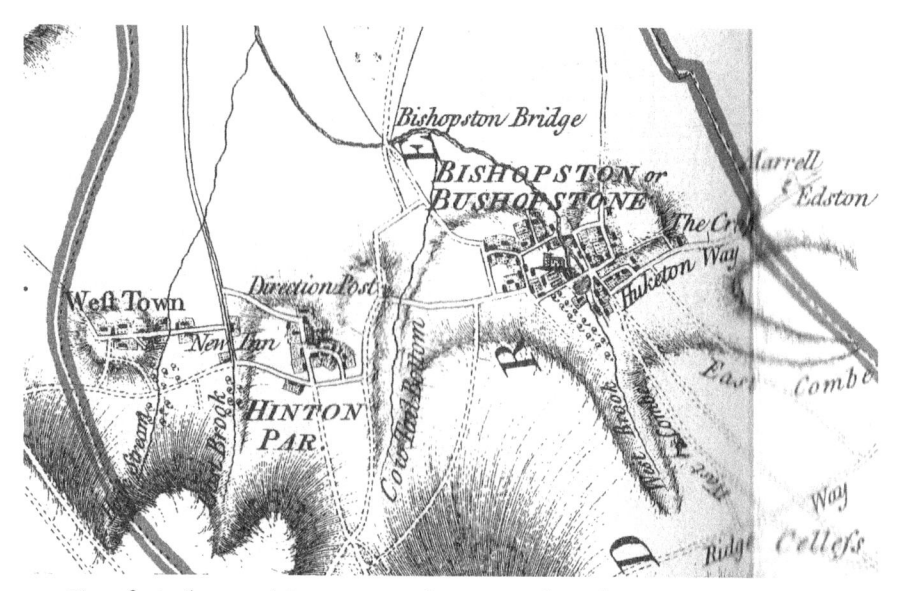

Fig. 46. Andrew and Dury's map of 1773 (Local Studies, Swindon Libraries)

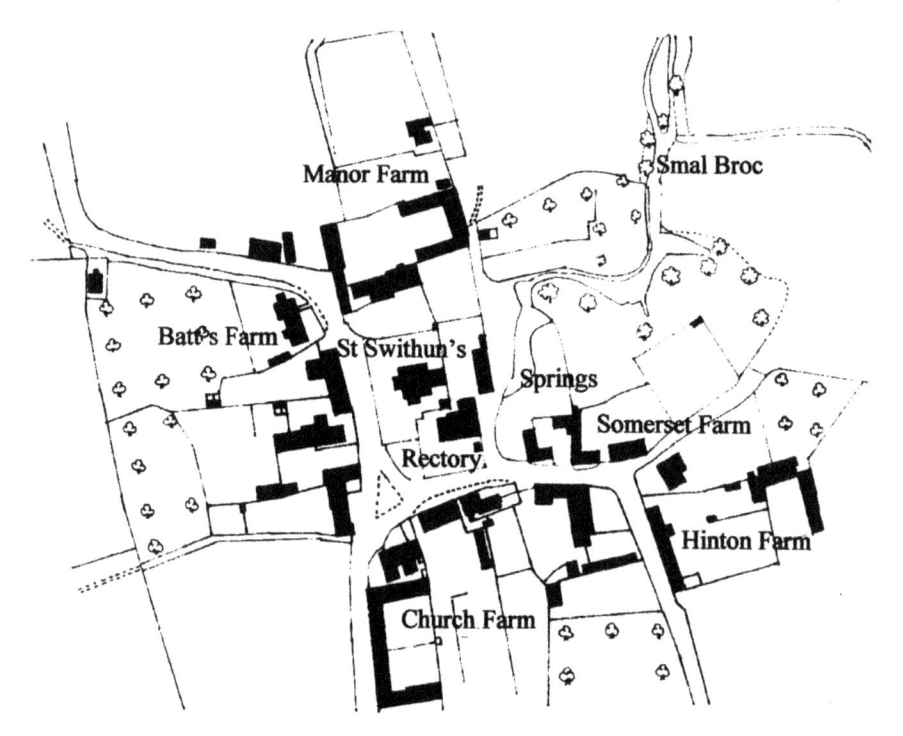

Fig. 47. Little Hinton c.1890 showing the five farms that constituted the village

with barley, 125 acres with oats, 344 acres with peas, beans, and vetches, 49 acres with clover and ryegrass, and 512 acres were fallow. It seems likely that in the 18th century the number of farms fell and that their sizes increased, but the amount of subletting makes that impossible to prove. In the 19th century and early 20th century Starveall and Ridgeway were smaller upland farms, but since the Second World War there have been only three principal farms in the parish – Manor, Prebendal and Eastbrook, of which Manor and Prebendal have sometimes been held together. Watercress was cultivated in beds north and south of Bishopstone Mill from 1878, or earlier, until the 1930s, or later. There have been occasional references to cloth working in Bishopstone and in 1927 hemp was said to be produced commercially.[45]

Little Hinton Parish's contribution to 16th-century taxes, in particular the benevolence of 1545 and the subsidy of 1576, were among the smaller ones made by the places in Elstub Hundred in which the village lay. The parish had 143 inhabitants in 1700. The Census of 1801 recorded 239 people living in Hinton, a figure that gradually increased until 1851 when the population numbered 354. Although numbers thereafter generally declined slight increases were seen in 1891 and 1911. In 1931 208 people lived at Hinton.

In 1638 there were two commons – The Marsh and Lambslade – which were shared between the *demesne* farmer and the copyholders. In 1659 the down fields south of the village – the Reeve lands, The Marsh, East Mead, and the open fields below the hill in West Hinton – were inclosed by agreement between the *demesne* farmer and the tenants. Farmer Francis Hungerford was allotted 115 acres and the eighteen copyholders a total of 523 acres. At least some of the land in East Hinton was re-allotted in 1787 when the East and West fields there, which contained 410 acres, were inclosed. The demesne farmer then received 248 acres, and of the nine copyholders in the tithing John Anger received 76 acres and John Woodward 49 acres. The open fields of West Hinton, the West, East, and North fields below Coombe, the West and East fields above Coombe, and New England, which contained a total of 450 acres were, with certain old inclosures, allotted by agreement in 1821. Six tenants in the tithing received allotments and the largest of 259 acres was made to Thomas Evans. Little re-arrangement of the farms within the manorial estate took place until the later 19th century. By 1896 the area of Manor Farm had been reduced to 169 acres by the creation of a hill farm of 609 acres worked from Hill Manor. The area of West Hinton Farm had by then been reduced to 20 acres. After 1879 the Ecclesiastical Commissioners' land in the parish formed a farm of over 200 acres[46].

A shaped eighteenth- century boundary stone, noted in a hedge in the coomb south of Hinton, bears the carved letter S and is a marker delineating the edge of Somerset Farmland.

Several substantial farmhouses, once attached to copyhold farms within the manorial estate, cluster on either side of the village lane that forms a northern loop from the Wanborough to Bishopstone road. Two, which have thatched roofs and are partly timber-framed, are probably of seventeenth century origin. Others are externally of late eighteenth or early or nineteenth century date and have walls of chalk blocks, many apparently re-used, with brick dressings. Of Hinton's outlying farmhouses Mount Pleasant Farm and Hinton Marsh Farm to the north are respectively of earlier- and later nineteenth century construction. On the downs to the south Hill Manor appears to have been built in the later nineteenth century.

At Erlescote excavation and an archaeological watching brief were conducted during December 2000 and January 2001. It revealed several ditches, wall footings, postholes and rubble associated with Ashton Keynes ware and brick fragments, dating to the post medieval period.

Fig. 48. Boundary stone marked with the letter S near Little Hinton

Mills

The mill building near the centre of Bishopstone was said in 1788 to house two water grist mills. It was rebuilt by the lessee, Peter Knight, in 1818. The building's frontage, on the main through road, is very deceptive appearing as a single storey and an attic. However, from the rear it can be seen to be a three-storey building, plus the attic. Fed by a large mill pond on the opposite side of the road it was in 1864 said

Fig. 49. Bishopstone Mill building, dated 1818

to house three pairs of stones and in 1886 was a flour mill. Milling was apparently stopped between 1903 and 1907.[47] An excavation trench dug by the authors at the eastern end of the mill exposed the remains of the iron mill wheel and the edge of the wheel pit's stone walling. Examination of eighteenth and nineteenth century parish maps showed that an earlier mill had existed a little further to the east. Consequently, a small test pit dug a little to the east and to a depth of 0.70m exposed brick walling. A slight curve in the wall suggested that this might be the edge of a mill leat, whilst the size of the bricks hinted at a seventeenth-century or earlier construction.

A rent charge book of 1840 and a field map of 1885 referred to and located three fields – 'Further Mill Piece', 'Hither Mill Piece' and 'Mill Bank'[48] – within the former Little Hinton Parish. It is of note that the parish boundary described in the spurious Saxon Charter of AD 853 as extending along the *Smal Broc* deviates around 'Further Mill Piece' and 'Hither Mill Piece' that lie on the stream's eastern side. The relationship between parish boundaries and watermills is important since special arrangements were frequently made to incorporate a mill and its watercourse within a particular land unit. Within the stream at this point traces of a sarsen stone wall or revetting and a substantial sarsen dam across the stream are visible. A survey of an immediately adjacent and seemingly associated earthwork showed that two phases of construction existed, the primary being modified by means of the cutting of an extensive and deep hollow. To

Fig. 50. Remains of Bishopstone's Mill iron mill wheel and drive shaft

confirm the possible presence here of a mill small trenches were cut by the authors in 2001.[49] Two were cut within the hollow, one opposite the dam in the stream and the other on the edge of an apparently revetted channel at the northern edge of the hollow base. Both trenches produced pottery, metalwork and clay pipe fragments that showed the hollow had been partially infilled and the site abandoned c. 1660-70. Also found was a large amount of iron slag. Inclusion of chalk fragments in the slag hint that this derived from iron smelting in the near vicinity. The trench next to the dam revealed, aligned with it, and sitting on the natural bedrock, the lower course of a wall built of sarsen, chalk, and sandstone blocks. A shallow gulley lay between the wall and a compacted chalk floor or yard surface. From the gulley came a late medieval ceramic ridge tile fragment, a sherd from a Rhenish bellarmine salt glazed jug and three sherds of glazed earthenware, which date wise point to a sixteenth century to mid-seventeenth century for the gulley's infill. The other trench showed that a wall of large sarsen stones had lined the edge of a water channel. It is clear from the archaeological evidence that this earthwork is the location of an undershot mill of medieval date, perhaps earlier. Subsequently it was replaced in the late medieval or early post-medieval period with a more efficient overshot mill, achieved by cutting the hollow and erecting a new mill building that enabled water to flow onto the wheel top.

Several documents, dating to the eighteenth century refer to a mill- Cuttle Mill – as being adjacent to a ½ acre close known as Somerwell.

ITS ARCHAEOLOGY AND HISTORY

It is also recorded that the mill lies on the northeast boundary of East Hinton adjoining the Lordship of Little Hinton. Both facts favour 'Mill Bank' as being 'Cuttle Mill'. The dating evidence provided by the ceramic material, however, conflicts with the documentary date for the site's demise. The latest finds following demolition of the building are datable to 1660-70. That 'Cuttle Mill' is noted as a grist mill in an eighteenth-century document (WRO 700/187) implies that the mill is still operational and is not a reference to an area of land where a building

Fig. 51. Remains of the stone dam across the Smal Broc at Mill Bank, Hinton

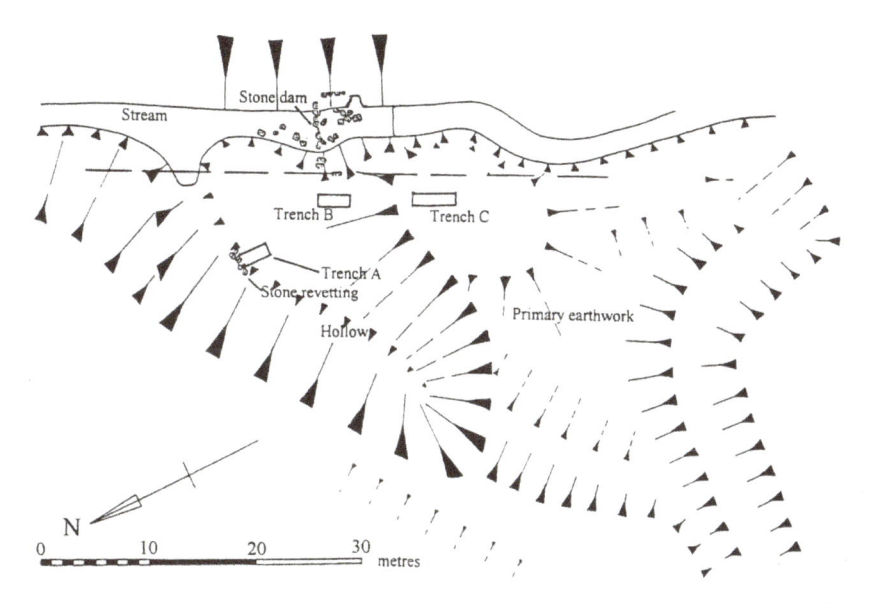

Fig. 52. Earthworks at Mill Bank, Hinton, and location of the excavation trenches

A Mill	Cuttle Mill	Berry/Bury Mill
Near Hinton Marsh Farm	May have been in East Hinton on northeast parish boundary	Attached to manorial estate with 17acres on north east parish boundary - southeast of Hinton Marsh Farm
1248 mentioned on the manorial demesne 1273 repaired 1280 House repaired 1281 Leased for 10 years		
		1419 mentioned
	16th century leased. Winchester Chapter to Waldron 1583, a 75acre farm leased with same	16th century held by Berry family
		17th century held by Berry family
	Late 18th century mill & farm Woodward family	1773 Andrews & Dury Map 15 1793 Whitworth Map
1840 Millbank leased16	1845 J Tucker tenant 1846 J Tucker tenant 1856 J Tucker tenant 1879 surrendered to Winchester diocese	Early 19th century Lea family 1820 Greenwood Map 1840 Hatt miller J Tucker copyholder 1861 Spindloe miller 1879 surrendered to Winchester diocese

Fig. 53. Records of Mills in Little Hinton Parish (various sources)

had formerly stood. The identification of the site as 'Cuttle Mill' is as a result uncertain, but unlikely on the present evidence. Cuttle Mill was leased by Winchester Chapter to the Walrond family in the later sixteenth century. From about 1583 a farm of 75 acres, was leased with it. In the later eighteenth century mill and farm, then usually leased for 21-year terms, were tenanted by the Woodward family. In 1845 John Tucker (d. 1856) was tenant and he was succeeded by his brother Thomas (d. 1868). The mill is last specifically mentioned in 1859 but may have fallen into disuse long before. In 1879 John Tucker's surviving devisees surrendered the property to Winchester Chapter's successors, the Ecclesiastical Commissioners, in whom the reversion had become vested in 1861[50].

Further north, a little south of Hinton Marsh Farm, a mill is evidenced on an Ordnance Survey map of 1829 and by remnants there of a demolished nineteenth century brick-built structure and a leat's channelling.[51] Andrews and Dury's map of 1773,[52] nevertheless, positions a mill north of the lane adjacent to the farm, presumably therefore a predecessor of the mill to the south, which was built on map evidence early in the nineteenth century. It is recorded that Hinton Marsh Farm, and so perhaps the first mill, suffered a disastrous fire at the beginning of the nineteenth century. Documentary evidence shows that the mill located here was, in the sixteenth and seventeenth centuries, held by the Berry family and in the later eighteenth century and the earlier nineteenth century by the Lea family. John Tucker became copyholder in 1845 and the mill thereafter passed like the Cuttle Mill estate and was absolutely surrendered to the Ecclesiastical Commissioners in 1879. Seventeen acres of land were attached to it[53].

North of Little Hinton Manor, archaeological observation of the cutting of a narrow trench by machine revealed nineteenth century pottery, tile, brick and glass fragments, and traces of flint cobbling[54]. In a nearby flower bed iron slag had been noted previously like that discovered on the nearby 'Mill Bank' earthwork site in a mid-seventeenth century context (see above).

Fig. 54. Overgrown brick channelling of the leat bringing water to Berry Mill, Hinton

Home Guard

In Tudor times each village was responsible for maintaining the necessary arms to defend themselves (the Home Guard), and this was known as the furnishing of harness. Muster commissioners would inspect the harness that could include long bows, bills, salets (helmets), brigandines (torso armour) and gorgets (neck and shoulder protectors). The muster roll records who possessed the arms, and also often added was the value of land or value of goods held by the other residents of the village who were liable to provide financial support if necessary (unfortunately not for Bishopstone). There were two main arms used in this period the bill (a long pole tipped with an iron point and an axe like blade on one side) and the long bow. Below is the 1539 muster of men aged 15 to 60 years in the Tything of *Bysschoppyston*.

Name	Armour and weapons
John Gregory	longbow
Roger Maddeley	longbow
John Mottorde	bill
Wyllyam Skatysby	bill
Willyam Lovelay	bill
Thomas Kempe	bill
Thomas Horton	bill
Wm. Spense Wyke	bill
Willyam Hall	bill
John Lacy	bill
Wm. Walter	bill
John Palmer	payre of splynts
John Precy	harnes
Robte. Tuctar	harnes
Wm. Cheppeman	harnes
Robte. Smyth	halfe a harnes
Wyllyam Hardyng	salett and gorgett
Wyllyam Kechen	sorde & a dagger
Wyllyam Hull	body of the harnes
Thomas Vycars	body of the harnes
Willyam Blakegrove	body of the harnes
Wm. Walter	body of the harnes

Fig. 55. The Tudor Muster of Arms at Bishopstone (Nick Boon)

Civil War

The English Civil War (1642 to 1651) seems to have largely passed Bishopstone and Little Hinton Parishes by although undoubtedly the villagers and farmers suffered from requisition and looting of food supplies and the loss of manpower as labourers and others joined the various armies. It is recorded that in 1643 traders heading for nearby Highworth's cattle market were experiencing great difficulties due to Royalists quartered in the area. Soldiers would simply take what they wanted in the way of corn and livestock. Oxen and horses had also become very scarce as they were needed as draught animals for pulling supply carts and cannon, or for the latter as mounts for the cavalry. Within St Swithun's Church at Hinton a gravestone records the burial of Thomas Wallrond in 1653. Thomas was the son of John Wallrond who at the time appears to have owned Hinton Farm. Before this the Wallrond family had resided in Hinton Manor Farm. The gravestone

Fig. 56. The gravestone of Thomas Wallrond, 1653

records that Thomas was....

> Of noble birth and that he was a pious and a wise soldier in his duty of bearing arms of war in the service to the Commonwealth until his death.

It would seem that the gentry of the village were supporters of Parliament during the war which gives credence to the local legend that the manor kitchen was the headquarters of the local 'Roundheads'.

Disastrous Fire
On Good Friday in 1891 at around 8pm a fire broke out in the tower of Bishopstone Church. The village had its own fire engine which bore the date of 1690. It had no hoses, just a brass nozzle that could be swivelled through a comparatively small arc and its water supply was usually carried in a canvas tank as the suction pipe was only sixteen feet long. It was operated by eight or ten pumpers under the direction of a captain who controlled the nozzle whilst standing on top of the appliance. At the time of the fire, it was captained by the village tailor John Povey. Many villagers along with the old fire engine attended the fire but the old engine proved of little use as it was not powerful enough. A messenger was sent to the nearest telegraph office at Shrivenham, and the Swindon Fire Brigade was cabled. They arrived just after 10pm and they immediately directed efforts on saving the tower where the fire was raging, whilst villagers removed items from the nave including the pulpit and an organ. After several hours, the fire was extinguished and the Swindon fire engine left. However, the towers belfry; its peal of bells that dated to 1620; the ancient tower clock and the roof were destroyed as well as part of the nave roof. Indeed, the heat had been so intense that the bells had completely melted. Early on Sunday morning the vicar (Reverend Herbert Ault) held communion in the church chancel for 84 communicants, a service that they would surely never forget. Subsequently services were held in the village school until the church was fully restored in 1893. The total cost of the restoration was £2,649-10s-3d (about £332,000 today) which included a new peal of bells and roofs for the tower and chancel. Money was raised through: insurance; subscriptions; donations and local events, including the selling of honey from the bees residing in the chancel roof.[55]

Post Medieval pottery

Ploughed fields around both Bishopstone and Hinton have produced evidence of former cultivation and the spreading of farmyard waste and night soil in the form of numerous seventeenth to nineteenth century pottery sherds and clay pipe fragments. Other finds we have made include a gun flint, an iron belt buckle and a mid-seventeenth century farthing token.

Pottery vessels such as plates, bowls, dishes, jugs, and chamber pots used during the first two centuries of the post medieval period were chiefly made in lead glazed redware. Potters recorded in the Ashton Keynes parish records seem to have been the main producer of redware for the region. Clearly, they were continuing the exceedingly long tradition of pottery manufacture in North Wiltshire. Seventeenth- or eighteenth-century kiln remains and discarded misfired pottery reject fragments have been discovered within a ploughed field on the edge of the village. Production at Ashton Keynes continued till the late eighteenth or early nineteenth century. In addition, early post medieval pottery found in the locale included, in relatively small quantities, Surrey green-glazed whiteware, Cistercian ware, and salt glazed wares from Raeran in Germany.

Fig. 57. Seventeenth/Eighteenth century pottery sherds, with wasters, from the Ashton Keynes kiln site

The seventeenth century saw the arrival of West Country sgraffito decorated red wares, delftware from London and Bristol, lustre stoneware from Nottingham and a variety of German stoneware's.

Feathered slip ware appeared early in the eighteenth century at a time which also saw major changes in pottery glazes and designs. White salt glazed ware developed by Staffordshire potters in 1720 brought about the demise of delftware and was itself replaced by creamware produced by Josiah Wedgwood in 1760. In 1779 Wedgwood also invented pearlware that soon ousted creamware. Production of English porcelain commenced in the mid-eighteenth century with factories at Worcester, Bow, Liverpool, Caughly and later at Plymouth and Bristol. The following century saw pottery mainly composed of plain, transfer printed or hand painted pearlware. Sherds of these various wares found include plates, saucers, tea bowls, coffee cans, teapots, coffee pots, jugs, bowls, chamber pots, tankards, and ornaments.

Clay Pipes

A few clay pipe fragments found in the parish bear their maker's name or mark. These fragments reflect the trends in pipe smoking and the local changes in pipe style during more than three hundred years. Tobacco smoking was introduced into Britain during the 1560s, but it remained very much a luxury until the turn of the century. Then it rapidly gained popularity despite the efforts of James I to tax it out of existence. In 1637 to achieve more control on tobacco importation and gain more revenue Charles I appointed Lord George Goring and his son George, Sir Drew Deane, and Sir John Latch to act as King's agents for the selling of tobacco licences. By the turn of the century the cost of tobacco was significantly reduced, enhancing its popularity, and encouraging makers to produce pipes with larger bowls. Pipes first entered the region, in small quantities, from the early pipe making centres of London, Bristol, Salisbury and Amesbury. Encourage by a growing popularity for smoking pipe makers began manufacturing in Marlborough around the middle of the seventeenth century. Strong competition occurred, however, at the end of the century from makers who had begun pipe production at East Woodhay in Hampshire and to a lesser degree by pipemakers from Ashton Keynes, Malmesbury, Cirencester and Devizes. Pipe makers largely confined their sales to a twenty- or thirty-mile radius from their workshops, the distance convenient for distribution by pack horse or cart. It is likely that makers sold their produce chiefly through tobacconists, inns, or alehouse, while some may have been sold in the markets or hawked from door to door. Decline in the popularity of tobacco smoking, as snuff taking found favour in the third quarter of the eighteenth century, saw the demise of the Marlborough, Malmesbury and Ashton Keynes pipe making industries. At East Woodhay production continued into the nineteenth century. Later pipes largely came from makers in Bristol, Broseley in Shropshire, Basingstoke, and Salisbury.

Initially pipes were small, but as the cost of tobacco fell the bowls became larger and the stems longer. An important change in pipe style in the southwest of the Country is considered to have been conceived by Thomas Hunt, a Marlborough pipemaker, in about 1685 and was quickly taken up by the other makers in the region. Pipes now had a spur beneath the bowl rather than a heel. Makers mark previously stamped on the heel were now impressed on top of the stem, close to the bowl's rear and, consequently, could be easily seen, even when using the pipe. Although the change occurred quickly amongst existing pipemakers the practice of giving apprentices, who had finished their time, an old pipe mould meant that the heeled pipes lingered on amongst these former trainees till about 1700.

Recorded marked pipe stems from the parish include RP, Thomas Hunt, Richard Cvtts, Thomas Widdos, and IF. Heeled pipes impressed RP are thought to have been made, c.1660-c.1690, by a Salisbury maker, pipes so marked being common there. Thomas Hunt pipes are found on both heeled and spurred pipes. Working c.1660-1691 he became a burgess of Marlborough and had a son who he named Thomas (working c.1690-c.1730). Thomas senior appears to have been born at Norton St Phillip in 1639 and had learnt the trade from his pipe-making father Jeffery Hunt, prior moving to Marlborough c.1660. The variety of stamps employed to mark the Thomas Hunt pipes vary greatly, as do the bowl forms and size. Their pipes are quite common and are found throughout Wiltshire and as far away as Gloucester, Bristol, Bridgwater, Barnstaple, Shaftsbury, Oxford, Southampton, and London. Working at East Woodhay/Boldre, Hampshire (c.1690-d.1731) Richard Cvtts married a Mary Harris in 1693 and they had seven children. His pipes

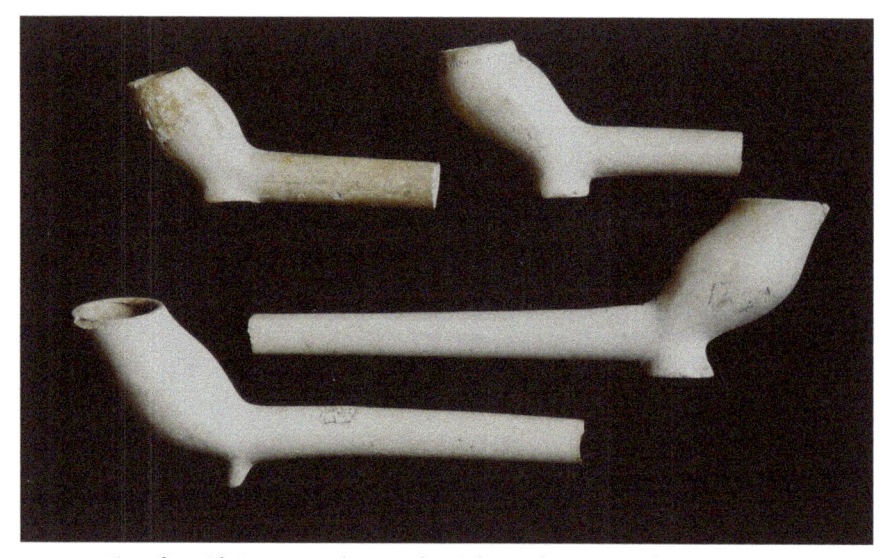

Fig. 58. Mid-Seventeenth to early Eighteenth-century clay pipe bowls

have been found in northeast Wiltshire, Berkshire, and Hampshire. Thomas Widdows, working *c.*1700-d.1729, initially worked at East Woodhay and is then recorded in 1718 at Marlborough. He appears to have moved back to East Woodhay shortly before his death. Also called Thomas a son, by his first wife Alice, appears to have continued to produce pipes. Their pipes are largely confined to North Wiltshire, South Gloucestershire, and West Berkshire. Pipes marked on the stem I.F are attributable to the maker John Foster of East Woodhay who was manufacturing pipes *c.*1720-c.1740. Pipes so marked been also found at Swindon, Highworth, Coleshill, Marlborough, Newbury, Chilton Foliat, Cricklade and Salisbury.

13
Undated Earthworks and Cropmarks

Well, here we are almost at the end having jotted down more than twelve thousand years of the Parish's archaeology and history as we know it. We hope you have enjoyed discovering about its origins, the changing landscape, its people, and their way of life. But before we finish there is one more chapter we ought to note down – the mysterious bits we do not yet have an answer for.

Many features such as earthworks or cropmarks, existing within the landscape cannot, without archaeological excavation, be firmly dated. These are to be found all over the parish on clay land, Upper Greensand, and chalk land by walking across fields and examining aerial photographs. To the experienced eye they show as lumps and bumps in pasture, parch marks on grass, patterns in growing crops or soil discolouration in ploughed fields. Some are immediately identifiable as to function and period, especially when associated with datable artefacts, others without further examination are not and a few will always remain a mystery. These features upon discovery need to be recorded to enable future research on them and to give them a degree of protection where necessary.

Within the parish such features are fairly numerous and mostly comprise of crop marks which have been recorded through aerial photography. For example – aerial photography has revealed east of Charlbury Hill an extensive double ditched or palisaded hexagonal shaped enclosure that straddles the Ridgeway. Its function and dating are a mystery. North of Lower Farm a large square enclosure is defined by its ploughed out outer bank and ditch. A possible entrance in the NE corner has a possible hollow-way extending southwards from it to another enclosure. Again, function and date for these remain unknown.

A few features comprise of surviving earthworks. One of these set on a high point west of Russely Park is a large square ditched enclosure. Set within it is another square ditched enclosure set slightly off centre. Its possible identification ranges from an ancient signal station to a former tree plantation. It also overlies an earlier boundary ditch that turns at ninety degrees beneath it, and which is identifiable as an earthwork in nearby pasture and discolouration in an adjacent ploughed field. Another feature lies southeast of Hinton Marsh Farm. Here part of an ovoid ditched enclosure is visible as a dark cropmark in a ploughed field. Divided by a hedge line the rest of the enclosure is defined in the adjacent unploughed grassed field as a wide shallow curved ditch.

North of Bishopstone Church a spring fed watercourse was diverted from its original route to the Smita stream. This diversion can be traced by map evidence to before 1758. Extending northwards after 400m the stream drops in level via two small man-made stone-built dams. At this point, in the eastern bank, traces of chalk block walling are evidenced. Could these remains imply the former presence here of an undershot mill? Only archaeological investigation will, perhaps, provide an answer.

14
The End, or is it?

Although this book records our present knowledge of the Parish's archaeology, it is really a never-ending story. Much more will undoubtedly be exposed during construction or will be turned up by the plough in years to come. However there comes a point in time that there is a need to put on paper for others, information that we have accumulated before we down trowels and hang up our muddy boots. But before then you may well see two ghostly figures looking down construction trenches and roaming fields in the search for traces of the people that walked these lands long before us.

Further Reading

Crowley, D. A. (edit.), 1980: 'Little Hinton' *Victoria County History of the Counties of England, A History of Wiltshire*, volume XI, pp 159-165, The University of London Institute of Historical Research, Oxford University Press

Elrington, C. R., 1983: 'Bishopstone', *Victoria County History of the Counties of England, A History of Wiltshire*, volume 12, pp 3-12, The University of London Institute of Historical Research, Oxford University Press

Knopp, Dorothy S. 1995 *Bishopstone, the Great Storm of 1932*, privately printed

Parker, Gwen. I. (rep.) 2007 *An Introduction to the History of Bishopstone*, privately printed

Williams, A. 1913 *Villages of the White Horse*, The History Press

Williams Paul A. 2010 *Little Hinton, Wilts*, privately printed

Williams Paul A. 2012 The History of the Church of St Swithun's, Little Hinton, privately printed

Wilson, R. H.1970 *Just for a Lark*, privately printed

Wilson, R. H. 1975 *The Sparrow Hunters*, privately printed

Online

Phillips, B. and Boon, R. Archaeological Sites in the Parish of Bishopstone & Hinton Parva – phillipsandboonarchaeology.neocities.org

Glossary of Terms

Blade – stone (flint, chert etc.) flake that have been removed from a core that has a length more than twice its width.

Burghal Hidage – Anglo-Saxon document providing a list of over thirty fortified places, the majority being in the ancient Kingdom of Wessex, and the taxes assigned for their maintenance.

Campanulate – bell shaped.

Carucate – area a plough team of eight oxen could till in a single annual season.

Chape – metal point of a scabbard.

Close – small, fenced field, usually lies near to habitation.

Copyholder – person who holds land according to the custom of the manor.

Core – piece of raw stone from which flakes, blades or bladelets have been removed.

Cortex – outer skin of a nodule of raw flint.

Demesne – land attached to a manor and retained by the owner for their own use.

Denarii – small silver coin of the Roman period, replaced in the third century with the *siliqua*.
Devisee – person who receives a gift of real property by a will.
Distal end – opposing end of a stone flake to the proximal end; i.e. the end directly opposite the platform.
Fabricator – finger shaped tool with at least one flat side, possibly used in the manufacture of leather items.
Flake – general term for all fragments that have been removed from a stone core. It may be intended for making into a tool, or just debitage.
Free warren – type of privilege conveyed by a sovereign to a subject, promising to hold them harmless for killing game of certain species within a stipulated area, usually a wood or small forest.
Furlong – unit of measurement equivalent of one eighth of a mile.
Grog – pellets of fired clay added to potting clay as temper.
Inclosed – any land which is surrounded by a fence, wall, hedge etc.
Hundred – sub-division of a shire.
Mortarium – bowl gritted internally for the grinding of herbs and spices using a pestle.
Mortlake – name given to a type of decorated Neolithic bowls.
Notch – small concave created by retouch on the edge of a flint flake or blade.
Overshot mill – mill where the water flows onto the top of the mill wheel.
Perpendicular period – the final phase of Gothic architecture in England, and it lasted from the late 14th until the early 16th century. The chief characteristic of Perpendicular architecture is the emphasis on strong vertical lines, seen most markedly in window tracery and wall paneling.
Platform – flat, natural, or prepared surface on a stone core which is struck by a hammer or punch to remove flakes.
Quern (rotary) – pair of circular stones, set one upon the other. The upper most having a central hole through which grain is poured whilst it is rotated so that the grinding process between the two stones produces flour.
Retouch – modification of a stone flake or blade to make a tool. Normally this takes the form of flakes or chips being removed from an edge and therefore shows as a series of regular negative scars on the edge.
Ridge and furrow – medieval strip fields.
Sarsen – sandstone blocks found in quantity on Salisbury Plain, the Marlborough Downs, in Kent, and in smaller quantities in Berkshire, Essex, Oxfordshire, Dorset and Hampshire. They derive from eroded silicification affecting beds of sand in Tertiary geological formations that overlaid the chalk.
Sheepcote/sheepfold –enclosure or building for penning of sheep.
Sherd – fragment of a pottery or glass vessel.
Slag – vitreous mass left as a residue by the smelting of metallic ore.
Stater – Iron Age gold coin.

Sunken featured building – structure constructed within a purposely dug flat bottomed hollow the base of which was used as the floor, or the hollow was floored over and the space created used for storage.

Tegula – Roman flat terracotta tiles having raised sides, used in conjunction with curved tiles (*imbrex*) for roofing.

Terret – metal loop on horse harness, guiding the reins and preventing them from becoming tangled or snagged.

Undershot mill – mill where the water flows against the bottom of the mill wheel.

Virgate – unit of land area measurement held to be the amount of land that a team of two oxen could plough in a single annual season (roughly thirty acres).

Wasters – Pottery rejects due to over-firing, distortion, or breakage on a kiln site.

Wildwood – a wood growing in its natural state, unaltered by human hand.

Yardland – another name for virgate.

Bibliography

Algar, D., Light, A. and Trehane, P., 1979 *The Verwood and District Potteries: a Dorset Industry* Ringwood

Anderson, A.S., 1978 *The Roman Pottery Industry in North Wiltshire* Swindon Archaeological Society Report No. 2

Anderson, A. S., Wacher, J. S. and Fitzpatrick, A. P., 2001 *The Romano-British 'Small Town' at Wanborough, Wiltshire* Britannia Monograph Series 19

Andrew, J. and Dury, A., 1952 *Map of Wiltshire 1773* Wiltshire Archaeological and Natural History Society Records Branch, Vol. VII, Devizes

Boon, R., 1999 *Bury Mill, Hinton Parva* GCE 'A' Level Thesis

Boon, R., 2000 *Archaeological Field Survey of 'Mill Bank', Little Hinton* coursework, University Oxford, Department for Continuing Education

Butler, C., 2005 *Prehistoric Flintwork* Tempus Printing ltd

Cannon, P., 1991 'Evidence of Tobacco Pipe Making in East Woodhay and District', *Transactions of the Newbury District Field Club* 14, no.1, pp 16-27

Cannon, P., 1995 'Further Evidence of Tobacco Pipe Making in East Woodhay and District', *Transactions of the Newbury District Field Club* no. 14

Coles, S., 2011: Medieval enclosures at Cue's Lane, Bishopstone, Wiltshire, *Wiltshire Archaeological and Natural History Magazine* 104, pp 151-165

Crittal, E. and Rogers, K. H. 1970 'Swindon', *Victoria County History of the Counties of England, A history of Wiltshire* 9, 104-168, The University of London Institute of Historical Research, Oxford University Press.

Crowley, D. A. (edit.), 1980 *Victoria County History of the Counties of England, A History of Wiltshire* XI, pp 159-165, The University of London Institute of

Historical Research, Oxford University Press

Cunnington, B., 1893 Notes on the discovery of Romano-British kilns and pottery at Broomsgrove, Milton, Pewsey, *Wiltshire Archaeological and Natural History Magazine* 27, pp 294-301

Currie, C. K., 1992 Excavations and Surveys at the Roman Kiln Site, Brinkworth, 1986, *Wiltshire Archaeological and Natural History Magazine* 85, pp 27-50

Draper, S., 200: Excavation and Fieldwork in Wiltshire 2007, *Wiltshire Archaeological and Natural History Magazine* 102, pp 331-345

Dunning, G. C., 1949 Report on the Medieval Pottery from Selsey Common, near Stroud, *Transactions of the Bristol and Gloucestershire Archaeological Society* 68, pp 30-44

Eames, E., 1991 Tiles in (edit) Saunders, P. and E: *Salisbury an South Wiltshire Museum Medieval Catalogue* Part 1, pp 93-139, Salisbury an South Wiltshire Museum

Elrington, C. R., 1980 'Bishopstone', *Victoria County History of the Counties of England, A History of Wiltshire* 12, pp 3-12, The University of London Institute of Historical Research, Oxford University Press

Fowler, P. J. and Walters, B. 1981 Archaeology and the Motorway, 1969-71, *Wiltshire Archaeological and Natural History Magazine* 74/75, pp 69-132

Gilchrist, R., 2012 *Medieval Life; Archaeology and the Life Course* Boydell Press

Gingell, C. H. and J. H., 1981 'Excavations of a Medieval 'Highworth Circle' at Stratton St. Margaret', *Wiltshire Archaeological and Natural History Magazine* 74/75, pp 61-68

Gover, J. E. B., Mawer, A. and Senton, F. M., 1939 *'The Place-Names of Wiltshire'* English Place-Name Society, XVI, Cambridge University Press

Hall, M., 1998: The Archaeology of the Ashbury to Bishopstone Pipeline, South Oxfordshire/Wiltshire, 1993, *Oxoniensia* LXIII, pp 199-220

Hayman. R., 2010 *The Green Man* Shire Publications

Larsson, L., 1989 Big Dog and Poor Man, Mortuary Practices in Mesolithic Societies in Southern Sweden, in Larsson, T., B. and Lundmark, H., (edit), Approaches to Swedish Prehistory: A Spectrum of Problems and Perspectives in Contemporary Research, *BAR International Series* 500, pp 211-223, Oxford

Lewcun, M., 1985 The Hunt Family Identified, *Society for Clay Pipe Research* Newsletter 8, 14-21

Lucket, L., 1970: Notes The Savernake Kilns, *Wiltshire Archaeological and Natural History Magazine* 65, pp 200-1

McCarthy, M. R., and Brookes, C. M., 1988 *Medieval Pottery in Britain AD 900-1600* Leicester University Press

Meekings, C. A. F., 1961 *Crown Pleas of the Wiltshire Eyre, 1249* Wiltshire Archaeological and Natural History Society, Records Branch, XVI, Devizes

Mepham, L. and Heaton, M., 1995 A Medieval Pottery Kiln at Ashamstead,

Berkshire, *Medieval Ceramics* 19, pp 29-43

Morris. J. 1979 *Domesday Book – Wiltshire* Phillimore

Musty, J., 1973 A Preliminary Account of a Medieval Pottery Industry at Minety, North Wiltshire, *Wiltshire Archaeological and Natural History Magazine* 68, pp 79-88

Myres, J. N. L., 1986 *The English Settlements* The Oxford History of England, 1986, Clarendon Press, Oxford

Pafford, J. H. P., 1953 The Spas and Mineral Springs of Wiltshire, *Wiltshire Archaeological and Natural History Magazine* LV, pp 1-29.

Passmore, A. P.., 1928 Fieldwork in North Wilts 1926-28, *Wiltshire Archaeological and Natural History Magazine* 38, pp 244

Payne, A., Corney, M. and Cunliffe, B., 2006 *The Wessex Hillforts Project* English Heritage

Pearce, J. and Vince, A., 1988 *Surrey Whitewares* London and Middlesex Archaeological Society, Special Paper Number 10

Pettitt, P., Bahn, P. and Ripoll, E., (edit.), 2007 *Palaeolithic Cave Art at Creswell Crags in European Context* Oxford University Press

Phillips, B., 1981 Starveall Farm, Romano-British Villa, *Wiltshire Archaeological and Natural History Magazine* 74/75, pp 40-55

Phillips, B., 2002 Excavation and Fieldwork in Wiltshire 2000, *Wiltshire Archaeological Magazine* 95, pp 291

Phillips, B., 2012 *Hinton Manor 2012: An Archaeological Watching Brief (HM12)* client report BP/HM2012

Phillips, B., and Boon, R., 2011 'Green Man Found on Tiles in St. Swithun's Church, *Village News for Bishopstone and Hinton Parva* February issue

Phillips, B., and Boon, R., 2013 *Goddard's Piece, Bishopstone, Wiltshire* Private publication

Phillips, B., and Boon, R., undated *'Millbank', Hinton Parva; a Mill Site?* Private publication

Phillips, B. and Walters, B., 1977 'A Mansio at Lower Wanborough, Wiltshire', *Britannia* 8, pp 223-7

Pugh, R. B., 1939 *Abstract of Feet of Fines Relating to Wiltshire for the Reigns of Edward I and Edward II*, Wiltshire Archaeological and Natural History Society, Records Branch I, Devizes

Rigby, V., 1982 'The Coarse Pottery', pp. 153-200, in Wacher, J., and McWhirr, A., Cirencester Excavations 1; *Early Roman Occupation at Cirencester*, Cirencester Excavation Committee

SMR Sites and Monuments Records, Wiltshire and Swindon Records Office, Chippenham, Archaeological Section

Swan, V. G., 1984 *The Pottery Kilns of Roman Britain* R.C.H.M. Supplementary Series

Thompson, T. R., 1959 'The Early Bounds of Wanborough and Little Hinton- An exercise in topography', *Wiltshire Archaeological and Natural History*

Magazine 57, pp 201-211

Vince, A G, 1997 'Excavations at 143-5 Bartholomew Street, 1979' in Vince, A. G., Lobb, S. J., Richards, J. C. and Mepham, L., 1997 *Excavations in Newbury 1979-1990* Wessex Archaeology mono 13, pp 7-85

Whittle, A., Healy, F. and Bayliss, A., 2011 *Gathering Time: Dating the Early Neolithic Enclosures of Southern Britain and Ireland* Oxbow Books

Notes

1　Crittal, E. and Rogers, K. H. 1970, 176
2　Gover, J. E. B., Mawer, A. and Senton, F. M., 1939
3　Gover, J. E. B., Mawer, A. and Senton, F. M., 1939
4　Crittal, E. and Rogers, K. H. 1970, 174
5　British Museum – Research
6　Current Archaeology
7　Current Archaeology, issue 247
8　Butler, C. 2005, 57-81
9　Pettitt, P. 2007
10　Phillips, B. 2012
11　Larson, L. 1989
12　Butler, C. 2005, 33-118
13　Whittle, A., 2011
14　Phillips, B., and Boon, R., 2013
15　Coles, S., 2011
16　Phillips, B., and Boon, R., 2013
17　Rudd, C., 2010
18　Robinson, P. R., 1977
19　Anderson, A. S., Wacher, J. S. and Fitzpatrick, A. P., 2001
20　Phillips, B. and Walters, B., 1977
21　Phillips, B., 1981
22　Pafford, J. H. P., 19?
23　Phillips, B., and Boon, R., 2013
24　Coles, S., 2011
25　Swan, V., 1984
26　Currie, C. K., 1992
27　Phillips, B., report in preparation
28　Hill 2003
29　WANHM 101, 275, WANHM 102, 332
30　Hayman, R, 2010
31　The Rectors Book, Bishopstone
32　Meekings, C. A. F. 1961, 173
33　Elrington, C. R., 1980

34	Meekings, C. A. F., 1961
35	Phillips, B., 2013
36	Elrington, C. R., 1980
37	Elrington, C. R., 1980
38	Crowley, D. A., 1980
39	Gingell, C. H. and J. H., 1981
40	Vince, A G, 1997
41	Mepham, L. and Heaton, M., 1995
42	Musty, J., 1973
43	Dunning, G. C., 1949
44	Pearce, J. and Vince, A., 1988
45	Crowley, D. A., 1980
46	Elrington, C. R., 1980
47	Crowley, D. A., 1980
48	Boon, R., 2000
49	Phillips, B., and Boon, R., undated
50	Elrington, C. R., 1980
51	Boon, R., 1999
52	Andrew, J. and Drury, A., 1952
53	Elrington, C. R., 1980
54	Phillips, B., 2012
55	The Rectors Book Bishopstone

People and Places Index

Illustrations are denoted by page numbers in italics

Acteon 34
Aethelred (King) 49
Alfred (King) 47, 48, *48*
Algar, Walter 59
Amesbury 82
Andrews and Dury, map 70, 76, 77
Anger, John 71
Angles 41
Anglo-Saxon 43, *45*, *45*, 46
Anglo-Scandinavian 49
Annales Cambriae 43
Artemis 34
Arthur 42, 43
Ashdown, Battle of 47
Ashton Keynes 81, 83
Ashton Keynes kiln 81
Ashton Keynes Parish Record 81
Ashton Keynes ware 72
Assandun (Ashingdon or Ashdon, Essex), battle of 49
Atrebates 28, 32
Atrebatic 28
Ault, Reverend Herbert 80

Badbury 43
Badbury Castle 43
Badbury Hill 43
Baddeburri (Badda's burh) 43
Badon Hill 43
Badon, Mount 42
Bagsecg 47
Barbury Castle (*Beranburh*), battle of 43
Barnstaple 83
Basingstoke 83

Bath 44
Beaker People 19
Beranburh (Barbury Castle), battle of 43
Berkshire 84
Berkshire, West 84
Berry family 76, 77
Berry Mill, Hinton 60, 76, 77
Bishopstone 1, 2, 4, 5, 9, 13, *31*, 36, 40, 53, 54, 59, 61, *62*, *62*, 64, 65, 68, 71, 72, 81
Bishopstone Church 5, 18, *22*, 55, 56, 66, 80, 86
Bishopstone Downs 29
Bishopstone Manor 3, 68
Bishopstone manor house 59
Bishopstone Mill 71, *73*, *74*
Bishopstone Parish 1, 53, 64, 79
Bishopstone with Little Hinton Parish 1, 30, 38
Black Death 60
Blacksmith 62, *63*
Blakegrove, Willyam 78
Boldre, Hampshire 83
Bone Hill 40, *45*, 46
Bordars (smallholders) 53
Bosworth Field, battle of 68
Bow 82
Boxgrove, West Sussex 7
Bridgwater 83
Brinkworth 37
Bristol 82, 83
Britain 7, *8*, 10, 11, *14*, 25, 41
Britannia Prima 33, 41, 43, 44
British 26, 41

Broomsgrove Farm 37
Broseley, Shropshire 83
Burhs 48
Bury Mill 76

Calleva Atrebatum (Silchester) 32
Camlann, Battle of 43
Canute 49
Catevaulauni 30
Caughly 82
Ceawlin 43
Celtic 39
Central Gaul 38
Charlbury Hill 15, 18, 46, 85
Charles I 82
Cheppeman, Wm. 78
Chichester 32
Chilton Foliat 84
China 60
Chippenham 47
Cirencester 37, 82
Cistercian ware 81
City Corner, Little Hinton 18, *21*, 23, 35
Claudius 30
Coarse Border ware 67
Coarse Border potteries 67
Colchester (*Camulodunum*) 30
Cole, River 1
Coleshill 84
Commonwealth 80
Constantine III 39
Convent of St Swithun's 2
Coombe field 71
Cornwall 32
Cottars (cottagers) 53
Creswell Crags 8
Cricklade 48, 50, 84
Crimea 60
Cues Lane, Bishopstone 13, 24, 36, 63
Cuttle Mill 74, 75, 76, 77
Cvnetio (Mildenhall) 28
Cvtts, Richard 83

Cynric 43

Danes 49
Danish 47
Dartford, Kent 7
Deane, Sir Drew 82
Delft ware 82
Demesne 61, 62, 63, 68, 71
Denmark 49
Deorham (Dyrham), battle of 44
Devizes 82
Devon 32
Dobunni 30
Dobunnic 28
Domesday Book 53
Dorchester 44
Dorset 38, 44
Downs Barn 23
Durocornovium 32, 41
Durotriges 32
Dyrham, South Gloucestershire 44

Earlscourt 1, 2, 50, 72
Earlscourt Farm 61
Early Norman 56
East Anglia 44, 47
East England 49
East field 71
East Hinton 71, 75
East Mead 71
East Wiltshire Tribe *28*, 28
East Woodhay, Hampshire 83, 84
Eastbrook Farm 71
Ecclesiastical Commissioners 77
Edington 48
Edmund II 49
Edward the Confessor 51
Edward the Elder 49
Elstub Hundred 71
England 49
England, Southeast 67
England, Southern 47, 49
English Channel 19

English Civil War 79
Ermin Street 32, 65
Ethandun, Battle of 48
Ethelwulf, King 1
Europe 4, 6, 7, 61
Evans, Thomas 71

Farmer(s) 53, 64
Fishbourne 32
Forest Hill 28
Forty Farm 36
Foster, John, of East Woodhay 84
Foxhill 18
Freeman 53
Further Mill Piece 73

Gaul, Central 38
Gaulish 41
German stoneware 82
Germanic 39, 41
Gildas 41, 42
Gloucester (*Glevum*) 32, 83
Gloucestershire, South 84
Gore Farm 18
Goring, George, junior 82
Goring, George, Lord 82
Gratian 39
Green Man 56
Greenwood, map 76
Gregory, John 78
Grove, Little Hinton 13, 24
Guthrum 47, 48

Halfdan 47
Hall, Willyam 78
Hampshire 84
Hampton 44
Happisburgh 7
Har Stan 50
Haradrada (King) 51
Hardyng, Wyllyam 78
Harley Bushes 23
Harlstone House, Bishopstone 45, 63

Harold Godwinson 51
Harris, Mary 83
Hart, miller 76
Hastings, Battle at 51
Henry VII 68
Henry VIII 68
Highworth 79, 84
Highworth Hundred 64
Hill Manor 72
Hinton 59, 71, 72, 81; *see also* Little Hinton
Hinton Copse 50, 53
Hinton Downs 1, 18, 23, 24, 27, 29, *31,* 35, 46
Hinton Farm 61
Hinton Manor 2, 17, 18
Hinton Marsh Farm 61, 65, 72, 76, 77, 79, 86
Hinton Parish 1, 50
Hither Mill Piece 73
Hoarder of St Swithun's 2
Hol Stan 50
Holocene 6
Holy Well 13, *35,* 35, 36
Homo antecessor 7
Homo heidelbergensis 7
Homo sapiens 7
Horton, Thomas 78
Hull, Wyllyam 78
Hungerford, Francis (farmer) 71
Hunt, Jeffery 83
Hunt, Thomas 83
Hunt, Thomas, junior 83

Icknield Way 1, 5
Industrial Revolution 68
Innkeeper 49
Ireland 6
Isle of Man 49
Isle of Wight 32
Ivar the Boneless 47

James I

Jutes 41

Kechen, Wyllyam 78
Kempe, Thomas 78
Kendrick, Matthew 3
Kennet Valley ware(s) 65, 67
Kent 44
Knight, Peter 72
Knights 51, 53

Lacy, John 78
Lambslade common 71
Lammy Down 24
Latch, Sir John 82
Late Medieval/Post Medieval 74
Late Saxon/early Norman 55, 58
Lea family 77
Legio II 30
Lenta 5, 24, 36, 50, 62
Liddington Castle 25, 27, 29, 42, 43
Liddington Parish 15, 64
Little Hinton 1, 2, 5, 7, 13, 31, 36, 40, 45, 53, 55, 56, 61, 62, 63, 64, 70, 72, 75; *see also* Hinton
Little Hinton Manor 9, 77
Little Hinton Parish 4, 71, 73, 76, 79
Liverpool 82
London 67, 82, 83
Lower Farm 85
Lower Wanborough (*Durocornovium*) 37
Luttrell Psalter 59

Maddeley, Roger 78
Magnus Maximus 39
Malmesbury 48, 50, 82, 83
Man, Isle of 49
Manor 59
Manor Farm 59, 71, 72
Marcus 39
Marlborough 28, 37, 82, 83, 84
Marsh Common 71
Marsh Mead 71

Martinsell 37
Medieval 57, 74
Medieval, Late/Post Medieval 74
Mediterranean 61
Medway, River 30
Mendip 9
Mercia 44, 47, 49
Mildenhall 28
Mill Bank 73, 75, 77
Mill Bank, Hinton 75, 75
Miller 60
Minety, North Wiltshire 65, 67
Minety/Selsley Common ware 67
Minister Commissioners 78
Minton 56
Moneyer 49
Mons Badonicus (Mount Badon) 42, 43
Mortlake pottery 18
Mottorde, John 78
Mount Badon 42, 43
Mount Pleasant *31*
Mount Pleasant Farm 36, 72
Muster of Arms 79

Neanderthals 7
Nennius 43
Newbury 84
New England field 71
New Forest 38
Norfolk 7
Norman 51, 55
Norman, Early 56
Normandy 49, 51
Normandy, William, Duke of 51, 53
Norse 47, 48, 49
North field 71
North Sea 47
North Wiltshire 81, 84
Northeast Hampshire 67
Northeast Wiltshire 65, 67, 84
Northeast Wiltshire Parishes 64
Northern Britain 47

Northern England 49
Northumbria 44, 47
Norton St Phillip 83
Norwegian 51
Nottingham lustre stoneware 82

Offa, King 44
Oldfield, John 3
Old Minster, Winchester, 2
Oxford 83
Oxfordshire 38

Pafford, J H P 36
Palmer, John 78
Parliament 80
Pictish 39
Plautius, General 30
Ploughman 53
Plymouth 82
Potters 49, 81
Povey, John 80
Prebendal Farm 59, 71
Precy, John 78
Pytheas 26

'R P' (pipemaker) 83
Raeran salt glazed wares 81
Ralph of Hinton 60
Ralph the Bishopstone Miller 59
Ramsbury 2, 3
Ramsbury Hundred 2
Reeve lands 71
Rhenish 74
Rhineland 38
Richard III 68
Richborough, Kent 30
Ridgeway 5, 27, 29, 43, 47, 85
Ridgeway Farm 71
River Cole 1
River Medway 30
River Thames 5, 28, 48
Rogues Road 5
Roman 39, 43, 47, 48

Roman Empire 32
Romano-British 42
Rome 30, 39
Roundheads 80
Russley 69
Russley Downs 12, 13, 24, 27, 28, 68
Russley Park 29, *31*, 34, 46, 85

St Mary's 53, 54, 57
St Swithun's 36, 45, 53, 55, *56*
St Swithun's Church 57, *58*, 79
St Swithun's, Convent of 2
St Swithun's Priory 55
Salisbury 56, 82, 83, 84
Salisbury Museum 15
Savernake Forest 28, 37
Saxo-Norman 50
Saxon(s) 41, 43, 44, 45, 46
Saxon Charter 73
Saxon, Late/early Norman 55, 58
Scandinavians 49
Selsley Common, Gloucestershire 65
Shaftesbury 83
Shepherd(s) 60, 64
Shepherds Steps 64
Shopkeepers 49
Shrivenham 80
Sidford, Mr F 18
Silk Road 60
Skateholm, Sweden 10
Skatysby, Wyllyam 78
Slave 53
Smal Broc 5, 73, 75
Smita (River Cole) 1, 50, 86
Smithy 62, *63*
Smyth, Robte 78
Somerset 44, 48
Somerset farmland 72
Somerton 44
Somerwell Close 74
South Gloucestershire 84
Southampton 83
Southern Britain 29

Southeast England 67
Southern England 47, 49
Southern Europe 25
Spindloe, miller 76
Staffordshire potters 82
Stamford Bridge 51
Starveall Farm *31, 32, 33, 33, 34,* 65, 71
Stratton Park 65
Suetonius 30
Surrey green-glazed whiteware 81
Surrey/Hampshire border 67
Svein Forkbeard 49
Swindon 84
Swindon Fire Brigade 80

Thames Estuary, Greater 14
Thames, River 5, 28, 48
The Marsh common 71
Tostig 51
Tottenham House, Great Bedwyn 37
Tucker, John 76, 77
Tucker, Thomas 77
Tuctar, Robte 78
Tudor 54, 68, 78, 79
Tything of *Bysschoppyston* 78

Ubbe Ragnarsson 47
Uffington Castle 29
Upper Thames Valley 14

Vespasian 30
Victorian 56
Villeins (villagers) 53
Vycars, Thomas 78

Wallingford, Oxfordshire 48
Wallrond, Thomas 79, 79
Wal(l)rond family 76, 79
Walter, William 78
Wanborough 59, 72

Wanborough Parish 2, 15, 18
Wanborough Warren 18
Wantage, Oxfordshire 47
Wedgwood, Josiah 82
Wessex 1, 44, 47, 48, 49
Wessex School tilery 56
West Berkshire 84
West Country sgraffito 82
West field 71
West Hinton 71
West Hinton Farm (*Westhyneton*) 63, 72
West Surrey 67
West Swindon 37
Western Britain 43, 47
Westminster Abbey 51
White Hill 18
Whitehill Farm, West Swindon 37
Whitworth, map 76
Widdows, Alice and Thomas, 84
Wight, Isle of 32
William Duke of Normandy 51, 53
Wilton 44, 59
Wiltshire 44, 48, 83
Wiltshire Crown Pleas 60
Winchester 1, 2, 49, 59
Winchester, Bishop of 55
Winchester Chapter 76, 77
Winchester Diocese 76
Winchester, Old Minster, 2
Winchester Priory's estate, Wroughton 61
Woodward, John 71
Woodward family 77
Worcester 82
Wroughton 61
Wyke, Wm. Spense 78

York 47